Napoleon Hill's
KEYS TO
SUCCESS

Napoleon Hill's
KEYS TO SUCCESS

Foreword by W. Clement Stone

PIATKUS

© 1994 by The Napoleon Hill Foundation

All rights reserved

First published in 1994 by
Dutton, an imprint of Dutton Signet,
a division of Penguin Books USA Inc.

First published in the UK in 1995 by
Piatkus Books Ltd
5 Windmill Street, London W1T 2JA

Reprinted four times

This edition published 2004
Reprinted 2004

The moral right of the author
has been asserted

A catalogue record for this book is
available from the British Library

ISBN 0 7499 2528 0

Edited by Matthew Sartwell

Set in Palatino
Printed and bound in Great Britain by
Bookmarque Ltd, Croydon, Surrey

CONTENTS

INTRODUCTION

You can achieve success in anything you do, and this book will show you how to do it.

Napoleon Hill's Keys to Success is the most practical and revealing examination of the Seventeen Principles of Success that Napoleon Hill ever wrote. These seventeen principles are the essence of the action and attitudes of everyone who has ever had a lasting accomplishment. If you make them your actions and attitudes, you will realize every one of your worthwhile goals.

The Work of a Lifetime

Andrew Carnegie, the founder of a steel corporation that later helped form U.S. Steel and a great philanthropist, charged the young Napoleon Hill with what was to be his life's work: the assembling and analyzing of the qualities that had allowed the great figures of the early United States to achieve their lasting success. Armed only with introductions from Carnegie and a fierce determination, Hill set out to interview more than five hundred of these titans and distill their philosophies into a logical framework.

From men such as Henry Ford, Thomas Edison, Woodrow Wilson, and later Franklin Roosevelt, Hill gained invaluable insights. He also learned about the limitations each faced: He found Ford personally insufferable; he encountered and understood Edison's struggles with near deafness; and though he worked hard for FDR during the Great Depression to combat the national malaise, he disagreed strongly with many of the President's programs. Hill believed they placed too little emphasis on individual effort and lured Americans into relying on others, instead of on themselves. But by observing, working, and talking with these people, Hill learned priceless lessons that were much greater than the sum of his subjects' accomplishments.

Though Hill had already published a number of books which revealed his findings in broad detail and enjoyed commercial success, his crowning achievement was the publication of the all-time best-selling business inspirational book *Think and Grow Rich* in 1937.

This clear, concise elucidation of the way to success was an immediate sensation. It lays out the techniques of personal achievement in everyday language, full of examples and exhortations. More than fifty years later, supported by the work of the Napoleon Hill Foundation, Napoleon Hill's masterwork still finds thousands of new admirers every year, people whose lives are infinitely changed for the better.

Hill continued to refine his philosophy, sharpening his focus as his wisdom grew and as he met even more people whose lives had been built on the ideas he had outlined. The major outlet for his new knowledge was a veritable whirlwind of speeches, lectures, and articles he prepared over the next thirty years. He spent his life spreading the gospel of success as directly and as personally as he could.

Unfortunately so much of the additional intelligence that Napoleon Hill developed was not published in book form. While he persisted in speaking all through his vigorous retirement, the hundreds of thousands of people who discovered *Think and Grow Rich* after Hill's death in 1970 have not had the advantage of his guidance on the many more practical points he pursued after the book was written.

With this in mind, the trustees of the Napoleon Hill Foundation directed that the key elements of Hill's later inspiration be set forth in this book.

A New Work

Napoleon Hill's Keys to Success gives you direct, simple, even brilliant advice on implementing the Seventeen Principles of Success, the major idea behind *Think and Grow Rich* and the focus of Hill's lifetime of study. With it you will see how to focus your ideas and enthusiasm into a coherent, comprehensive plan for prosperity.

The techniques for applying the seventeen principles, the methods by which you can develop them, and the practical insight into their influence on your life all are here just as Napoleon Hill laid them out.

The text of the book is Hill's own, compiled from manuscripts, lectures, and college course materials he wrote. The only addition to Hill's work is the inclusion of some contemporary examples of the seventeen principles in action. Because Hill's wisdom was so universal and enduring, the benefits of following his advice are just as easily demonstrated in your lifetime as they were in Hill's. The hazards of ignoring the seventeen principles are also still all too easy to see. They're included, too.

Napoleon Hill's Keys to Success then, is vintage Napoleon Hill, direct, straight-talking advice in the manner of the backwoods Virginia boy who became a confidant of Presidents and the prophet of a uniquely American philosophy of achievement.

It will offer you lucid instruction, keen insight, and a host of opportunities to improve your situation and become a better, more valuable person as you do so. As you read, keep ever in your mind Napoleon Hill's fundamental maxim, the keystone of all his thought, and you will experience the rewards of success as surely as millions have before you:

WHATEVER YOUR MIND CAN CONCEIVE AND BELIEVE,
YOUR MIND CAN ACHIEVE.

◆ 1 ◆
DEVELOP DEFINITENESS OF PURPOSE

A Valuable Secret
◆
The Advantages of Definiteness of Purpose
◆
The Power of the Subconscious
◆
Putting Definiteness of Purpose to Work
◆
Creating a Plan
◆
Success Is a Worthy Goal
◆
Creating Opportunity

Your progress toward success begins with a fundamental question: Where are you going?

Definiteness of purpose is the starting point of all achievement, and its lack is the stumbling block for ninety-eight out of every hundred people simply because they never really define their goals and start toward them.

Study every person you can think of who has achieved lasting success, and you will find that each one has had a definite major purpose. Each had a plan for reaching that goal, and each devoted the greatest part of his or her thoughts and efforts to that end.

Andrew Carnegie was the man who led me to formulate my definite major purpose: assembling and publicizing the principles by which great individuals achieve enduring success. Carnegie started work as a laborer in a steel mill. Because of his definite major purpose to make and market better-quality steel than anyone else, he became one of the wealthiest men in the country and was able to endow libraries in small towns all across America. His definite major goal was more than a wish; it was a *burning desire*. Only by finding your own burning desire will you achieve success.

The difference between a wish and a burning desire is crucial. Everyone wants the better things in life—money, fame, respect—but most people never go beyond just wishing for them. If you know what you want from life, if you are determined to get it to the point that it becomes an obsession, and you back that obsession with continuous effort and sound planning, then you have awakened and developed definiteness of purpose.

A Valuable Secret

The most important part of this book is not written on its pages but is already in your own mind. Once you learn how to harness the tremendous potential of your mind and how to organize the knowledge you already have, you can turn them into the power necessary for attaining your definite major purpose.

There is a proverb which says:

"If you would plant for days, plant flowers.
If you would plant for years, plant trees.
If you would plant for eternity, plant ideas!"

This book has been written to induce a flow of ideas through your mind. It will introduce you to your other self, the self which has a vision of your innate spiritual powers and will not accept or recognize failure. It will arouse your determination to go forth and claim the things which are rightfully yours.

As Ralph Waldo Emerson wrote, "One single idea may have greater weight than the labor of all the men, animals and engines for a century." Put ideas and your definiteness of purpose to work.

The Advantages of Definiteness of Purpose

Definiteness of purpose develops self-reliance, personal initiative, imagination, enthusiasm, self-discipline, and concentrated effort. All these are required for success. Throughout this book you will learn in greater detail just what these qualities entail and how they are acquired, developed, and incorporated into your plan for success.

Definiteness of purpose also brings a host of other advantages.

Specialization

Definiteness of purpose encourages you to specialize, and specialization leads to perfection. Your success in life will depend a great deal on your ability to know much about a specific area and to perform exceptionally within it. General education is important because by pursuing it, you will discover your basic aptitudes and desires. Once you have discerned them, however, you should immediately begin to acquire specialized knowledge in your major interest. Definiteness of purpose will act as a magnet to attract to you the specialized knowledge necessary for success.

Budgeting Time and Money

Once you have determined your definite major purpose, you will begin to budget your time and your money and all your day-to-day endeavors so that they will lead to the attainment of your major purpose. Time budgeting always pays dividends because each moment is made to progress toward your goal. Money is also used to its best advantage, ensuring that you pass the mileposts along the road to success.

Alertness to Opportunity

Definiteness of purpose makes you aware of opportunities related to your major purpose, and it inspires the courage to act on them.

Edward Bok was an immigrant to this country who set out to make his living by writing. He began a flourishing business writing short biographies, which employed six people. One evening at the theater he noticed that the programs were large and cumbersome, poorly printed, and unattractive. On the spot he conceived the idea of producing a smaller program, easier to hold, better-looking, and including appealing reading matter. The next morning he prepared a sample copy of his proposed program and presented it to the theater manager. Not only would he provide the theater with a better program, but he would do it free in exchange for the exclusive rights. Advertising would pay his costs and bring him profit. The theater agreed, and Bok went into partnership with a friend more experienced than he in publishing and advertising. They quickly signed up all the other theaters in town to avoid competition. The business thrived and eventually expanded to create several other magazines, while Bok became the editor of the *Ladies' Home Journal*.

If you can see an opportunity as quickly as you can see the faults of others, you will soon succeed.

Decision-Making Capability

Successful people make decisions quickly (as soon as all the facts are available) and firmly. Unsuccessful people make decisions slowly, and they change them often. Remember that ninety-eight out of a hundred people never make up their mind about their major purpose in life; they simply can't make a decision and stick to it.

How can you overcome the habit of avoiding decisions? Start with the very next problem you face, and make a decision. Make *any* decision. Any decision is better than none. If you make some mistakes at first, take courage: Your batting average will improve. Knowing what you want will help in decision making, of course, because you can always judge whether or not it will contribute to your goals.

Cooperation

Definiteness of purpose develops confidence in your own integrity and character, which attracts favorable attention from others and inspires their cooperation.

Those ninety-eight folks who can't determine their major goal will be inspired by one who can. And those few who, like you, have embarked on their journey, will recognize and want to aid a fellow traveler.

Faith

The greatest benefit of definiteness of purpose is that it opens your mind to the quality known as faith. It makes your mind positive and frees it from the limitations of doubt, discouragement, indecision, and procrastination.

These limitations are some of the greatest roadblocks you will face. Later chapters will specifically address overcoming them, but possessing faith in yourself and in the fact that the universe is constructed to allow you to achieve your greatest potential will help you—starting now.

Success Consciousness

Closely related to faith is success consciousness. Your mind becomes sold on success and refuses to accept the possibility of failure.

A young man lived in Salt Lake City many years ago. He was industrious, thrifty, and much admired. Then he did something which convinced his friends he had taken leave of his senses: He withdrew all his money from the bank, went to an automobile show in New York, and returned with a new car. Worse, as soon as he got home, he put that car in his garage, jacked it up, and proceeded to take it apart, piece by piece. After examining every piece, he put the car back together again. The folks who were watching him thought he was just plain wacky. They were further convinced he was mad when he began the process again, and again and again.

That man was Walter P. Chrysler, whose innovations revolutionized the automobile industry. There aren't any major corporations or skyscrapers named for his Salt Lake City neighbors, who lacked the insight to see the method in his madness. They had never heard of definiteness of purpose, and they couldn't recognize how success consciousness destines a person for success.

The Power of the Subconscious

Any dominating idea, plan, or purpose held in your conscious mind through repeated effort and emotionalized by a burning desire for its realization is taken over by the subconscious and acted upon through whatever natural and logical means may be available.

The only thing over which you have complete right of control at all times is your mental attitude. "Right of control" means that you *can* control it; it does not mean that you do control it. You must learn to exercise this right as a matter of habit.

The conscious mind is where reasoning and thinking occur. It analyzes information and data, and it acts as a guardian of the doorway to the subconscious. The conscious mind develops as a result of experience. The subconscious mind does not think, reason, or deliberate. It acts instinctively in response to basic emotions. The differences in people are due to the ways they have trained their conscious minds; subconsciously we all are very much alike.

The subconscious can be compared with a car, while the conscious mind can be considered the driver. The power is in the car, not the driver. The driver must learn to release and direct that power.

The subconscious mind receives any image that is transferred to it by the conscious mind under strong emotion. Think of the pair as a camera: The conscious mind acts as a lens, concentrating the image of your desires and bringing them to a point on the film of the subconscious. Getting good pictures with this camera is the same as it is with any other: The focus must be sharp, there must be good exposure, and the timing must be right.

Correct focus requires a clear definition of purpose. The composition of the photo must be made with care and precision; *you* decide what to include in the frame. The proper timing is determined by the intensity of your desire at the moment of exposure. Experienced photographers rarely take just one shot of an important image; they work at it again and again until they get the photo they want.

This sort of repeated exposure of the subconscious to the image of your desire is crucial. You must work at the process repeatedly until you have transferred the exact image you want into your subconscious mind.

Don't be afraid of working yourself up into a highly emotional state when you are impressing images upon your subconscious. When your purpose is a worthy one, you don't need to fear this type of autosuggestion. The intensity with which you impress your subconscious with a picture of your plan directly affects the speed with which the subconscious will go to work to attract the picture's physical counterpart by inspiring you to take the right steps.

Putting Definiteness of Purpose to Work

Making your subconscious work for you is only the first of many steps. You will not succeed if you cannot convince other people to cooperate with you and if you do not live in accordance with strict standards. Those standards form the remainder of this book.

But let's assume you have developed the necessary definiteness of purpose. You are now likely to ask an obvious question: Where do I get the resources to implement my plan?

The first step from poverty to riches is the most difficult. The key is to realize that all the riches and all the material goods that you acquire through your own efforts begin with your having a clear, concise picture of what you seek. When that picture grows to be an obsession with you, you will find that your every action leads you toward its acquisition.

Andrew Carnegie's life again provides an excellent example. Once he knew he wanted to make steel, he fed that desire until it was the driving force in his life. He then turned to a friend, similarly broke but smart enough to recognize that value of his idea. Because he was impressed by the power of Carnegie's obsession, the friend joined forces with Carnegie. Their combined enthusiasm was sufficient to convince two others.

These four people became the nucleus of Carnegie's empire. They formed a mastermind group, the subject of the next chapter. Together they were able to find the capital necessary to pursue Carnegie's obsession, and each of them made a vast fortune as a result.

It was not sheer hard work that made these men successful. You probably know several people who work as hard as you do at anything they try—perhaps even harder than you—and are never successful. Education isn't the reason either. Sam Walton never won a Rhodes scholarship, but he made more money than anyone who ever studied at Oxford.

Great success is the result of one's understanding and using a positive mental attitude (PMA). Your mental attitude gives power to everything you do. Having a positive mental attitude means that your actions and thoughts further your ends; having a negative mental attitude means that you are constantly undermining your own efforts. As you build your desire into an obsession and develop definiteness of purpose, you will also build and develop your positive mental attitude.

It would be foolish to suppose that having developed your definiteness of purpose and PMA, you will immediately find that you have the resources you need. The speed at which you acquire these will depend on the size of your needs and on the control you exercise to keep your mind free of fear, doubt, and self-imposed limitations.

If you need ten thousand dollars for your definite major purpose, you may be able to marshal it in a few days or even hours by impressing others with the quality of your enthusiasm and vision. If you require one million dollars, it's likely to take longer.

An important variable in this process is just exactly what it is you offer in exchange for that ten thousand or one million dollars. The time required to deliver the service or the equivalent value you intend to supply is also significant. You must be clear about what it is that you will *give* before you can expect to *get* in return.

Creating a Plan

No one gets something for nothing. People who have money to give will expect to receive something in return: a product, a service, an increase in their own capital. You will not be successful overnight; in fact, you will not be successful until you have returned to everyone who has aided you everything that he or she is due. Your definite major purpose must include provisions for doing this.

You may be nodding your head in agreement with this and deciding you will surely make this happen. But unless you have an extraordinarily disciplined mind, it is not enough to envision this part and every other part of your plan. You must write them down.

Writing out your definite major purpose forces you to be specific about it. It reminds you of its strengths and will expose its weaknesses. If you cannot put what it is you are going to do into words, it's probably because you are not as sure about it as you think.

Once you have written your plan, read it aloud to yourself at least once every day. This fuels your obsession and reinforces its nature in your mind. When you face a choice about how to proceed, having your written definite major purpose to read will clarify your goals and make sure that you continue to progress toward them.

Even better, once you have assembled your mastermind group, you ensure that everyone stays focused on the same ends by use of a written plan. No single mind is complete; no one person can answer every question. But two or more minds, united behind a definite major purpose and working in harmony to achieve it, will accomplish great things.

There are numerous examples of this power. Christ himself made an alliance with his disciples to carry out his work. The plan was his own, but it survived betrayal and his absence to achieve a success beyond human comprehension.

Success Is a Worthy Goal

Striving for success has its detractors. Some people will argue that those who acquire wealth do so at the expense of the people who work for them. But if you are going to achieve success, you will do so only by extraordinary effort, effort that most people are not willing to make.

People seldom profit by having money unless they earn it. How many times have you read about lottery winners who find themselves bankrupt only a few years after their windfalls? Or about heirs to great fortunes, reared in atmospheres of indulgence, who fall prey to addictions like alcohol or gambling?

The value of the wealth that comes with success is that it carries with it the lessons you have learned in acquiring it. You will learn in achieving wealth that success comes about only because you are willing to assume great responsibility and to deliver unfailingly goods and services which are truly valuable.

Most people would not choose to be as dedicated to a definite major purpose as you must be. If you were to accumulate a fortune and then offer it to them on the condition that they behave exactly as you have done, most would not accept the responsibility. But some would.

It is the people who would make such a choice who will be most helpful to you. They can offer you aid of untold value, far above and beyond the efforts of those who are easily contented. They will become indispensable to you by their willingness to assume responsibility and relieve you of some of the load you are carrying. You must be willing to reward them generously for their efforts. People like this learn that they set their own salaries by the quality of their work.

Everyone, in fact, does the same. A person's salary is determined by the sort of service he or she renders—the quantity and quality of that service, plus the mental attitude under which it is rendered.

If millions of people are struggling to get by on the salaries they earn, it is because their highest aim is only to hold the jobs that they currently have. They are where they are, and they are making what they make, solely because of the limitations they have set up in their own minds.

Creating Opportunity

There is a theory which pops up again and again that the opportunities for success are fewer now than they were in the past, that our nation has reached the plateau of its success, that the world is dominated by people who already have money, and that success is a finite realm already filled to capacity.

This is nothing more than a theory. There is no scarcity of opportunity. There is only a shortage of imagination. Countless people gain new wealth every year, whether the economy is prospering or ailing. The only limits they recognize are those within their own minds. Anyone who cries "no opportunity" is simply issuing an alibi for his or her own unwillingness to assume responsibility and use imagination. Offering a useful good or service is just as valuable now as it ever was, and new areas in which to do so open up every day.

Consider Home Depot which stood the idea of the corner hardware store on its head by offering a huge selection of items at low prices. Bed, Bath and Beyond has done the same thing in its market. Robert Johnson founded Black Entertainment Television, targeting a market that the major networks only served part of the time. All these were unusual ideas in their time. Yet they have been enormously successful in areas no one would have imagined a decade before.

There's a story about a congressman around the turn of the century who wanted to introduce a bill to close the Patent Office on the ground that there was nothing else to be patented; everything worthwhile had already been invented! If you laugh at that idea, then laugh again at anyone who tells you that the days of opportunity are over.

The pursuit of opportunity has given this country its strength. If you lose yourself in an obsessional desire to make yourself useful to others, you will find yourself through the recognition of the good you are doing. If you forget that you must make yourself useful to others, you will stray from the path to success, no matter how long you have already walked it.

Consider for a moment those great blue-chip companies, such as IBM, which have learned such a lesson at their peril. For years IBM made itself indispensable to business operators, large and small, by producing high-quality machines to run their offices. Then IBM turned its eyes only to making big, powerful computers, while its customers were looking for small, personal units for each employee. Profits plummeted, employees were laid off for the first time in company history, and IBM was faced with completely remaking itself in an industry it had once dominated.

What IBM lost was *the desire for knowledge and the willingness to earn it.* Its people had stopped wondering what it was their customers wanted, and they didn't bother to find out. Dozens of smaller computer manufacturers possessed of that quality stepped in and made fortunes. Write that quality into your definite major purpose, and never overlook its value.

Your achievements—like a company's—correspond unerringly to the philosophy with which you relate to others. If you follow through on your willingness to deliver scmething useful in return for what you seek, the world will be compelled to reward you on your own terms. Recognition of this fact is at the heart of what has made America great.

Our most precious natural resource is not our mineral deposits or our beautiful forests. It is the mental attitude and the imagination of the people of every generation who have mixed experience with education to deliver goods and services that improve the lives of both Americans and people around the world. Our real wealth is the intangible power of thought.

This is why definiteness of purpose heads the list of the seventeen principles you must master to achieve success. No one can be successful without first knowing what it is he or she wants. If this principle is to have any value to you, you must follow it as a daily habit.

If you still think that luck is a key to success, then you

have missed the point of this chapter. Some people do fall into opportunity, but they usually fall back out again. And if they do manage to retain their good fortune, it is only because they have worked just as hard to keep it as you must to acquire yours. And that calls for definiteness of purpose.

✦ 2 ✦
ESTABLISH A MASTERMIND ALLIANCE

Forming a Mastermind Alliance
✦
Maintaining Your Alliance
✦
Form a Mastermind Alliance with Yourself
✦
Cultivate Mastermind Alliances Wherever You Can

A mastermind alliance is built of two or more minds working actively together in perfect harmony toward a common definite object.

The mastermind principle lets you appropriate and use the full strength of the experience, training, and knowledge of other people just as if they were your own. You can overcome almost any obstacle you face, no matter what your own education or talents, if you use the mastermind principle effectively.

No one has ever attained outstanding success in anything without applying the mastermind principle. No one mind is complete by itself. All truly great minds have been reinforced through contact with others that allowed them to grow and expand.

Forming a Mastermind Alliance

For a model of a mastermind alliance at work, consider a train crew. The conductor (you) can take the train to its destination only because all the other members of the train crew recognize and respect his (your) authority. What would happen if the conductor failed to signal the engineer that it was time to start? Passengers would abandon the train and find some other way to get where they wanted to go. If the engineer didn't bother to heed the signals along the track, the resulting crash could cost lives.

For your mastermind alliance to function properly, you must give clear, unmistakable signals to your crew. They, in turn, need to be willing to cooperate fully with you. There are four simple steps to making sure this is the case.

Step One: Determine Your Purpose

The first step in putting together a mastermind alliance is to adopt a definite purpose for it to attain. (Who would board a train without knowing where it went?) Obviously you cannot do this if you have not yet selected your own definite major purpose. You must be certain that the purpose of the alliance is either the same as yours or very closely aligned.

If you have already written out your own definite major purpose and the means you will use to attain it, this step will be familiar for you. Writing out the plan for your alliance's success will make you aware of every one of the links of the chain you must forge. Inevitably there will be links you have neither the skill nor the resources to join yourself, just as the conductor cannot simultaneously collect fares, work the dining car, and keep a hand on the throttle. This brings you to your second step.

Step Two: Select the Members of Your Alliance

Choosing the people who will help you attain your goal must be done carefully. You may initially select some people who you later decide are not appropriate, and you may discover that there are unanticipated needs for knowledge that must be filled. Trial and error will be part of the process, but there are two qualities to keep foremost in your mind that will help you avoid too many surprises.

The first is *ability to do the job*. Do not select people for your alliance merely because you like and know them. Such people are valuable to you because they improve the quality of your life, but they are not necessarily suited to a mastermind alliance. Your best friend may not be the most knowledgeable marketing professional in your area, but perhaps he can introduce you to someone who is.

The other quality is the *ability to work in a spirit of harmony with others*. Without harmony your alliance will falter, perhaps not right away but at some crucial moment when everything is about to be won or lost.

Andrew Carnegie once told me of a worldwide search he conducted for his chief chemist. His scouts found a brilliant man working for a German firm. His ability was without question. Carnegie entered into a five-year contract for the man's services. Within a year he had released the man from the bargain.

Why? Because the chemist was so temperamental that he had an entire department in upheaval. None of the other chemists could work with him, and the fellow was so concerned with perceived slights that he spent all his time fuming and accomplished nothing.

You must keep any thoughts of discord out of your alliance. There must be a complete meeting of the minds, without any reservations on the part of any member. Personal ambitions must be subordinate to the fulfillment and successful achievement of the definite purpose of the alliance. This includes your own.

Being clear about your alliance's purpose will give you a basis for judging someone's ability to work in harmony with it.

You may still have to make adjustments in the alliance's composition, but there are also steps you must take to build that harmony.

Step Three: Determine Your Rewards

Clearly determined rewards for participation in your mastermind alliance are an important factor in its harmony. Determine at the outset what rewards you are offering in return for the work of others, and there will be little room for later recriminations.

There are ten basic motives toward action that can be the basis of these rewards:

1. Self-preservation
2. Love
3. Fear
4. Sex
5. Desire for life after death
6. Freedom for mind and body
7. Anger
8. Hate
9. Desire for recognition and self-expression
10. Wealth

Wealth will obviously have the greatest appeal for members of your commercial enterprise, but remember that other motives can play an important role. Recognition and self-expression are just as important as money to many people. Be aware that some of these motives—anger, hate, fear—can twist the minds of your team if you rely upon them.

Your best motivator, wealth, must be willingly, fairly, and generously divided among your team. The more generous you are, the more help you will get. Another of the principles of success is the habit of going the extra mile (see Chapter 5). It will serve you well if you incorporate it into your alliance from the beginning.

Step Four: Set a Time and Place for Meeting

Your alliance must be active to do any good. Establish a definite place and time for regular meetings to ensure that you are making progress and dealing with the issues you face. Your early meetings will likely involve fine-tuning the plan you have made for your success, drawing upon the specialized skills of your members.

As your alliance matures and harmony grows among the members, you will find that these meetings create a flow of ideas into every member's mind. As you work together over time, more excitement will greet every meeting, and more harmony will arise.

Think about a group of sales reps brought together for a conference. They may arrive in general agreement about their goals, but a day or a weekend spent reinforcing their determination, listening to and incorporating their suggestions for the plan at hand, will send them away fired up and eager to achieve their goals.

Do not let the regular meetings take the place of frequent contact between the members. Telephone calls, notes, and even conversations in a hallway will keep the alliance primed for action when it meets in full, so that sudden developments can be addressed quickly.

Maintaining Your Alliance

The harmony of your alliance is built upon the mutual agreement on your definite purpose. But like any construction, it must be preserved with diligent work. That work will be your task as its leader.

Your attention should focus on four areas.

Confidence

Confidence is reliance or trust based on proved fidelity, which means faithfulness to duty and loyalty to obligations. As the leader of the alliance you must inspire confidence in your members by your dedication to your definite major purpose. You must also insist within the group on confidentiality; often it is harmful for members to discuss the purpose of the alliance outside the group. Some people can give away a secret without a moment's thought; you don't need them in your mastermind alliance.

Understanding

All members of the group must possess a complete knowledge and comprehension of the nature, significance, and implication of a situation or proposition that the group faces. You may employ specialists to heighten your understanding of various fields, but every person involved must be able to deal with the core issues of every decision. And before a decision is made, each member of your group must be convinced that it is a good decision, one which he or she can support wholeheartedly.

Fairness and Justice

When you form your mastermind alliance, each member must agree at the outset on the contribution each will make toward your enterprise. Everyone should also be agreed on the division of benefits and profits. Everyone must deal with everyone else on completely ethical terms. No member of the alliance should seek unfair advantage at the expense of others. Otherwise dissension will arise and completely destroy the association.

Courage

Your alliance must meet danger and difficulties with firmness, resolution, and valor. The courage to do so comes from self-confidence and a well-developed success consciousness. The courage of two separate individuals is nothing compared with that of a united team, just as the power of a single battery is less than that of a group of batteries. This is another excellent example of the power a mastermind alliance derives from its harmony. The more the minds that are linked together, the greater the power harnessed, and the more the resistance that can be overcome.

Form a Mastermind Alliance with Yourself

A woman came to see me once and began to tell me all her difficulties. Her sight was almost gone, and she had given up on doctors, who she said were quacks. She had lost most of her money investing in movies, her husband was a philanderer, her mother had died after a long and awful illness, and her relatives were a plague. Her bitter catalog of woes went on and on, and if I hadn't felt sorry for her, I wouldn't have listened to them, she was so full of self-pity. Apparently not one good or constructive thing had passed her way in twenty years.

"Mr. Hill," she asked me, "why do all these things happen to me?"

I did not want to be harsh with her, but somehow I had to get her to face facts. I said, "Frankly, with your negative attitude it's a wonder that you are able to do anything at all. I'm not a bit surprised that your family bothers you or that your husband runs around. I'm amazed he hasn't left home!"

"What can I do to stop him?"

"You can't do anything for him now," I told her, "but you can do something for yourself. You've been thinking about your losses to the exclusion of everything else. The more you concentrate on them, the more you attract other losses. Stop thinking about them, make up your mind that you are going to benefit by your experience, and then adopt a definite plan for regaining your sight. Dwell upon the idea that your eyes will get better. Decide that you will seek medical help, and believe that it will work. If you can change your attitude toward yourself, your husband will see something to excite his interest in you again. Your relatives will stop seeing you as a doormat. I can't tell you any more than that now. When you manage to put yourself into a more positive frame of mind, come see me again. Before I do anything for you, *you must do something for yourself.*"

I tell this story because I want to say the same thing to you. Whatever personal obstacles you face, you must start getting to know that side of your personality that knows no obstacles, that recognizes no defeats. Cultivate a friendship with the "other" you, so that no matter what you are doing, you are allied with someone who shares your goals. All the philosophy and advice in this book about persuading and motivating others will be much more useful to you if you practice it on yourself.

If you have convinced yourself that you need and deserve a ten-thousand-dollar loan, you won't just walk into a bank and ask for it. You will cultivate the friendship and appreciation of the loan officer. You will present her with a list of the possibilities for the project you have in mind, you will outline your solid plans for repayment, and you will do it with infectious confidence. You will succeed.

You will begin to take charge of the efforts of others only when you take complete charge of the power of your own mind.

Cultivate Mastermind Alliances Wherever You Can

Once you recognize the benefits of mastermind alliances, you will understand that they can serve you in many areas.

You can—and must—make progress on many fronts to achieve personal success.

In Your Marriage

A mastermind alliance with the person you love most deeply is of untold importance. If you are married and have not built your relationship on the principles of harmony that are crucial to any alliance, you may have some reselling to do with your spouse. Set aside some time every day to talk about what you want to achieve and how you are going about it. Rely on your definiteness of purpose to build your persuasive abilities, to convince your partner of the benefits of the work you are doing. It is very unlikely that your plan will not affect your husband or wife in some significant way, and you absolutely must not drag your partner unwillingly into an adventure.

If you have embarked on your mission and the time comes that you are thinking of marriage, you must be very frank with your intended life partner about what you are doing and how you will do it. Build your mastermind alliance into your marriage from the start, and it will steady and support you through the darkest moments.

Indeed, your whole family should be incorporated into a mastermind alliance: your children, your parents, your siblings—anyone on whom you rely or who relies on you. Lack of harmony at home can easily spill over elsewhere; a united family is a great team.

In Your Education

No one's education is ever complete. You may rely on the specialized knowledge of others, but you should also learn from every possible source.

In this case your mastermind alliance is with the entire sum of human knowledge. You are united in the goal of increasing your understanding, and books, magazines, lectures, audiocassettes all are your allies. Make it a habit to read daily, not just newspapers, which merely keep you current, but materials which expand your mind; they will put you ahead.

The key to a mastermind alliance is the harmony of its members. You have to work constantly to strengthen the harmony of your many alliances. A crucial aspect of this effort is your ability to inspire harmony, which hinges strongly on the next principle we will explore: developing an attractive personality.

◆ 3 ◆

ASSEMBLE AN ATTRACTIVE PERSONALITY

Positive Mental Attitude (PMA)

◆

Flexibility

◆

Sincerity of Purpose

◆

Promptness of Decision

◆

Courtesy

◆

Tact

◆

Tone of Voice

◆

The Habit of Smiling

◆

Facial Expression

◆

Tolerance

◆

Frankness of Manner and Speech

◆

A Keen Sense of Humor

Faith in Infinite Intelligence

◆

A Keen Sense of Justice

◆

The Appropriate Use of Words

◆

Effective Speech

◆

Emotional Control

◆

Alertness of Interest

◆

Versatility

◆

Fondness for People

◆

Humility

◆

Effective Showmanship

◆

Clean Sportsmanship

◆

A Good Handshake

◆

Personal Magnetism

The third step in achieving lasting success is to develop an attractive personality. A pleasant personality is a well-rounded one; accordingly there are twenty-five different aspects of your personality which you must strive to improve. Don't be intimidated by that number, for you'll find that many of the aspects are closely related. Working to bolster one will help you strengthen many others.

Positive Mental Attitude (PMA)

A positive mental attitude is the right mental attitude in any given situation and is most often composed of the *plus* characteristics symbolized by such words as "faith," "integrity," "hope," "optimism," "courage," "initiative," "generosity," "tolerance," "tact," "kindliness," and "good common sense."

PMA is the most important aspect of any attractive personality; indeed, it is crucial to many of the Seventeen Principles of Success. PMA influences your tone of voice, your posture, your facial expressions. It modifies every word you say and determines the nature of the emotions you feel. It affects every thought you have and the results your thoughts bring you.

For the sake of contrast, let's examine the effects of a negative mental attitude. It dampens your enthusiasm, curtails your imagination, undermines your desire to be cooperative, overthrows your self-control, makes you sullen and intolerant, and, as if these weren't enough, throws your reasoning out of gear.

A negative mental attitude is so detrimental to your efforts that you are better off staying at home than venturing out into the world with it. It will only make you enemies and corrupt your good works and alliances. A lawyer who goes into court with the best case in the world will convince neither judge nor jury if her attitude is negative. What kind of confidence would you have in a sullen, pessimistic doctor, no matter how many degrees hang on the wall? None! People simply will not tolerate a bad mental attitude.

In contrast, a positive mental attitude opens doors and allows you to display your skills and ambitions. Imagine that lawyer presenting her case with confidence, gaining the ear of judge and jury because she is distinctively self-assured. Wouldn't you rather be treated by a physician who sets you at ease, answers your questions plainly, and demonstrates a knowledge of his field?

Building a positive mental attitude is part of the other aspects of an attractive personality. As you read on, you'll see how understanding and applying each of these points reinforces your PMA.

Flexibility

Being able to adapt yourself quickly to changing circumstances and emergencies without panic or loss of temper is a significant skill as you struggle toward success. Having a flexible disposition means you must be like a chameleon, quickly harmonizing with your environment.

This does not mean shedding your principles or altering your goals. A chameleon is still a chameleon regardless of whether it is brown or green. Flexibility means recognizing that your own mental attitude toward a situation determines if it is a disaster or a boon. If your product fails the first time out, is that good or bad? If you have flexibility, it's great. You have the opportunity to recognize flaws, to improve your product or its marketing early in the game. And because you have PMA as well, you are in an even better position to seize that opportunity.

Flexibility also means that in every negotiation you understand that the other party's needs and demands are ways in which you can better render the service you are offering in exchange. If someone needs your product a week before you have planned to deliver, you can recognize that he or she will not be the only client to make such a demand. Here, then, is your opportunity to discover how you can produce faster *and* better.

Sincerity of Purpose

There is no substitute for real commitment to your definite major purpose. Sincerity of purpose—or its lack—writes itself so indelibly into your words and deeds that anyone can recognize it. Insincerity is evident in your expressions, in your trend of conversation, in everything you do; no amount of acting skill can disguise it.

The yes-man is a universal object of derision precisely because everyone recognizes his insincerity. But if you are possessed of real sincerity of purpose, it will be just as visible. Andrew Carnegie told me once how he called a new employee into his office to issue a directive. The man listened, then looked him squarely in the eyes, and with a good-natured smile said, "All right, chief, you are the boss, but I'm going to tell you that your request is going to cost you money because you haven't investigated this matter as closely as I have."

Something about his assured manner, with no hint of insubordination, convinced Carnegie to delay his decision and investigate further. He discovered that he had been wrong and his new employee was right. That man was Charles M. Schwab, who eventually brokered the deal between Carnegie and J. P. Morgan that founded U.S. Steel. Schwab then went on to start up the mammoth Bethlehem Steel. He began his rise to prominence on the simple basis of his sincerity of purpose in everything he did.

Be sincere first of all with yourself, and you will steadily grow in self-reliance.

If you have sincerity of purpose, it will strengthen every one of the other aspects of your pleasing personality. What better compass could you have at a moment you must demonstrate flexibility than a true and lasting dedication to your definite major purpose?

Promptness of Decision

Dillydallying does not inspire popularity. In this fast-moving world, those who do not move quickly cannot keep up with the parade.

Successful people reach decisions definitely and quickly, and they become annoyed and are inconvenienced by others who do not. Prompt decision making is a habit, and it is supported by your positive mental attitude, which gives you confidence.

It is also closely tied to your sincerity of purpose; the more you are convinced of the value of your definite major purpose, the quicker you will be to discard distracting options and to select those which move you toward your goal. If your choice is between quick profit and a long-term relationship with a client, your sincerity of purpose allows you to make your decision quickly.

Opportunity is everywhere, but it is fleet of foot. Even if you have the vision to recognize it, without a fast decision on your part, it will be gone.

Courtesy

The cheapest and most profitable quality in the world is courtesy. It is absolutely free, save for the moments it takes to express it. Unfortunately, today it is also scarce, thus all the more valued when displayed.

Courtesy is nothing more than the habit of respecting other people's feelings under all circumstances, the habit of going out of one's way to help the less fortunate, the habit of controlling selfishness in all forms. Do not mistake high-flown manners for courtesy. Using the correct fork at dinner will do nothing to appease the company president whom you insult by dominating the conversation.

Courtesy demonstrates the self-awareness born of your positive mental attitude and projects the worthiness of your goals and proposals.

Tact

There is a right moment and a wrong moment for everything. Tact is the habit of doing and saying the right thing at the right moment. Tact is so closely related to courtesy that you cannot practice one without the other. It is an invaluable skill, just as noticeable for its absence as for its presence.

Here is a list of the most common ways people show their lack of tact:

1. Carelessness in their tone of voice, often speaking in gruff, antagonistic tones
2. Speaking out of turn, when silence would be more appropriate
3. Interrupting others who are speaking
4. Overworking the personal pronoun so that every sentence features the word "I"
5. Asking impertinent questions, often to impress others with their own importance
6. Injecting intimately personal subjects into the conversations when such subjects are embarrassing to others
7. Going where they have not been invited
8. Boastfulness
9. Flouting social norms in matters of attire
10. Making calls at inconvenient hours
11. Holding people on the telephone with needless conversations
12. Writing letters that are overly familiar to people they hardly know

13. Volunteering unsolicited opinions on any subject under the sun, without regard to their knowledge
14. Openly questioning the soundness of others' opinions
15. Declining requests from others in an arrogant manner
16. Speaking disparagingly of people in front of their friends
17. Rebuking people who disagree with them
18. Commenting on people's disabilities
19. Correcting subordinates and colleagues in the presence of others
20. Complaining when requests for favors are refused
21. Presuming upon friendship in asking for favors
22. Using profane or offensive language
23. Expressing dislikes at a drop of a hat
24. Dwelling on ills or misfortunes
25. Complaining about politics or religion
26. Displaying general overfamiliarity

If these faults seem small to you, consider how quickly they compound one another. Would you want to be associated with someone who displayed just three of them regularly? They reveal a lack of perception and careful consideration that undermines one's confidence in another's mental powers. Anyone who desires an attractive personality will avoid them all.

Tone of Voice

Speech is the method we use most often to express our personality. Controlling the tone of your voice so that it carries meaning beyond mere words is invaluable. You can say the same sentence in different tones of voice and convey very different things. "I need that shipment by Tuesday" can be pronounced with full confidence, letting your supplier know that your request is something you have every reason to expect as a normal part of your relationship. Say it anxiously, and you may find you've given him the idea that you're in a bind and perhaps he can demand a higher price. Say it angrily, and you can undo years of a good partnership.

Practice controlling your tone of voice, listening to the way you sound. When you speak confidently, your PMA and sincerity of purpose should show through.

The Habit of Smiling

Don't underestimate the importance of a frequent and sincere smile in making your personality appealing to others—or its effect on yourself. Try smiling the next time you're angry. This simple action is calming, and it's a reminder of the positive focus you want in your mental attitude. A smiling face defeats the cruelest of antagonists, for it is difficult to argue with someone who smiles while speaking.

Practice smiling in front of a mirror, preferably while working on voice control. The two aspects are related, both in the way others will perceive you and in their effect on your own actions.

Facial Expression

Here is another facet of an attractive personality that goes together with your tone of voice and your smile. You can tell a great deal about what is going on in people's minds by the expressions on their faces. Each of us makes judgments on this basis all the time; master salespeople are particularly good judges. The more you learn to be aware of and in control of your facial expressions, the better you will be able to interpret the expressions of others. And since you'll already be in front of the mirror to practice your tone of voice and smile, you'll have the perfect opportunity to develop this aspect as well.

Tolerance

Tolerance is the disposition to be patient and fair toward those whose opinions, practices, and beliefs differ from yours.

Holding your mind open to new ideas and new information is not simply a way to make yourself more pleasing to be around. Though it is closely related to tact as a social skill, tolerance makes you better able to identify and seize advantages. You may not make every new idea you encounter your own, but you will examine and try to understand it.

Intolerance brings a host of disadvantages:

1. It makes enemies of those who would like to be friends.
2. It stops the growth of the mind by limiting the search for knowledge.
3. It discourages imagination.
4. It prohibits self-discipline.
5. It prevents accuracy in thinking and reasoning.

The more intolerant you are, the more you close yourself off to the diversity of the world and to the power of the spiritual side of the mind, which can flourish only when it is ready to accept new ideas.

Frankness of Manner and Speech

Everyone resents people who use subterfuge instead of dealing frankly with associates. People who are so slippery that they cannot be pinned down to direct, clear-cut statements cannot be depended on.

The problem with these people is not that they lie outright but that they do what amounts to the same thing: They deliberately withhold facts from those who have a right to know them. This is base dishonesty, which undermines the soundest characters. Truly sound characters have the courage to speak and deal directly with people, and they follow this habit consistently, even though it may at times be to their disadvantage.

If you read about some of the earlier aspects and assumed that they could be used to engage in deceitful schemes, you are vastly mistaken. Without true frankness none of your other skills will be successful. If you have to resort to trickery, what kind of confidence do you have in your definite major purpose and what kind of attitude are you approaching it with?

A Keen Sense of Humor

A well-developed sense of humor aids you in becoming flexible and adaptable to the varying circumstances of life. It allows you to relax and remain human in the midst of pressure, instead of becoming cool and distant or angry and bitter. It keeps you from taking life too seriously.

People who cannot laugh when laughter is exactly what is called for are denying themselves a wonderful mental tonic. If you discover some flaw in your product or plan, recognizing the comedy of the situation allows you to back up and start again. Otherwise you will be trapped in your frustrations.

And a sense of humor makes the simple act of smiling so much easier and does wonders for your PMA.

Faith in Infinite Intelligence

Faith is woven into every principle of the philosophy of achievement; faith is the essence of every great achievement, no matter what its nature or purpose. Neglecting your faith while carrying out your definite major purpose would be like trying to study astronomy without referring to the stars. Faith is so important that it is actually one of the other Seventeen Principles of Success and will be covered in more detail in the following chapter.

Faith in Infinite Intelligence inspires faith in other human beings as well. Confidence begets confidence. Those who have faith in Infinite Intelligence, faith in themselves, and faith in others inspire others to have faith in them.

The greatest outlet for the expression of initiative, imagination, enthusiasm, self-reliance, and definiteness of purpose, is faith. The human mind is an intricate machine designed to accomplish things. The power that operates this machine comes from outside the mind, and faith is the master gate through which we gain full and free access to that tremendous power.

The mechanism which opens that gate is desire or motive. There is no other way to open the gate. It is opened by degrees, which are dependent on the intensity of those same motives and desires. Only a burning desire will open the gate to its fullest.

A burning desire is accompanied by deep emotional feeling. Sheerly logical motives do not open the gate as widely as those which spring from the heart.

Faith wipes out obstructions like intolerance by freeing your mind of human limitations. For what is intolerance but a closed mind? Just as darkness is dispelled by a simple light, so intolerance is eliminated by opening the mind to the influx of power that gives the brain the vision to encompass all of life's realities instead of just a few of them.

Faith provides us with the widest perspective on the world about us and the people who live in it. That perspective paves the way for a better understanding of all human relationships; thus faith supports all the traits of an attractive personality.

It also give us the power to see past worldly obstacles, to envision new solutions and new ideas on our paths to individual achievement. As one man has aptly stated, "Where faith is the guide, the individual cannot lose his way."

The power of faith is inexhaustible. It is the ultimate renewable resource, a reflection of the Creator's desire that we use it in every way possible.

Faith's power is easily attained by any person. No fee must be paid. It is simply appropriated through the desire for its use.

The only things over which you have complete control are your thoughts. The only real privacy you have is in your mind. It is there that you can make full and complete use of the power of faith to remove limitations from your mind.

A Keen Sense of Justice

Unless you deal justly with others, you cannot hope either to cultivate an attractive personality or to succeed in your definite major purpose. The essential component of a keen sense of justice is a dedication to intentional honesty.

Many people are honest for the sake of expediency, but this kind of honesty is so flexible that it can be contorted to serve in any situation which furthers their interests. By cultivating frankness of speech, you are already taking an important step in practicing intentional honesty; you must adhere to that honesty so closely that you practice it under any circumstance, whether or not it promises you any immediate gain.

Even if a keen sense of justice prevents you from seizing every opportunity, it carries with it a host of practical benefits:

1. It establishes the basis of confidence, without which you cannot have an attractive personality.

2. It builds a fundamentally sincere and sound character, which by itself is a powerfully attractive trait.

3. It not only attracts people but offers opportunities for real and lasting personal gain.

4. It builds your sense of self-reliance and self-respect.

5. It strengthens your relationship with your conscience and thus allows you to act more promptly since your motives and desires are clearer.

6. It attracts worthwhile friends and discourages your enemies.

7. It opens your mind to faith.

8. It protects you from destructive controversies. Consider how often people of prominence are laid low by revelations of impropriety.

9. It inspires you to move toward your definite major purpose with greater personal initiative.

A keen sense of justice is not merely a tool for gaining material rewards. It enhances every human relationship. It discourages avarice and selfishness and gives you a much better understanding of your rights, privileges, and responsibilities. With it, every aspect of an attractive personality grows stronger.

The Appropriate Use of Words

People who achieve success do it by careful and attentive effort. Your use of language must reflect this quality just as astutely as any marketing plan.

Do not make it a habit to litter your speech with curses, obscenities, or casual misusage. Instead work to make sure that you use words with precision and that they have the force and power to convey your meaning with all the clarity you desire.

If you are unsure of your language skills, you can improve them by reading. One man I knew read the dictionary for half an hour every day. Yes, he actually read the entries. I never heard him speak badly, and I was always impressed by the distinct messages he conveyed.

If this approach strikes you as too academic, consider the wide variety of self-improvement books and tapes which offer programs for vocabulary expansion. You cannot lose by increasing your mastery of language. Doing this will also rid your speech of clichés and other overused words which make your conversation leaden and induce sleep—not excitement—when you talk.

This skill is so important because people make many assumptions about you based on the way you speak and write. If your conversations and letters are direct, clear, and easily comprehended, all the other aspects of your attractive personality will be revealed much sooner and in much better light. And without the deft use of language, the harmony of a mastermind group will be disrupted by confusion over goals and the means for obtaining them.

Effective Speech

There is more to effective speech than the vital aspect of appropriate word choice. Combining frankness, word choice, and other aspects of a pleasing personality will make you a powerful communicator able to speak with conviction and persuasion, whether you are addressing a convention, a roundtable, or one person.

Dramatic, inspiring speech has had incredible influence on the course of civilization. The destiny of nations has been changed and defined by the power of those who know how to speak effectively, and those people have earned a permanent place in history. Your ambition may not be so grand— though why shouldn't it?

To master dramatic technique, you must learn to speak

forcefully in ordinary conversation. If you practice putting the necessary feeling behind every word you utter in every conversation you have, you will be much more effective in formal presentations.

No amount of dramatic technique, however, will bring an audience back from the dead. There's an adage: "Know what you wish to say, say it with all the feeling you command, and then sit down!" The last two words are the key here. Remember to keep your speeches short; as soon as you have conveyed your point, stop. Long-winded speakers tax the alertness of their audiences and show no respect for their time. They fail to persuade anyone.

You will fail just as surely if you do not focus your speech in a way that is applicable to your listeners. Do not use jargon or technical phrases with people who are new to your service or product. Remember that examples and illustrations add drama to your speech, and make your message hit close to home. If you are presenting a new computer system to a business that has never even used computers before, and you ramble on about LANs and Pentium chips, you will soon face a roomful of sleepwalkers. Tell them instead how you can link their employees together, how quickly information can be shared, and how fast and efficiently your technology will allow them to work, and you will face a roomful of people eager to do business with you.

As you speak, make good use of gestures. Avoid running your hands through your hair or shoving them in your pockets. Watch public speakers at every opportunity to learn how they employ their hands for emphasis, and practice this in front of a mirror, just as you practice your smile and facial expressions.

The effort you have devoted to controlling your tone of voice will pay off handsomely in your public speaking. You will convey enthusiasm, confidence, and importance through your tone of voice. Enthusiasm is the core element of any speech, for it underlies your ability to bring all the above aspects of good public speaking into a harmonious whole. It is very hard for listeners not to be affected by genuine enthusiasm; it is contagious. If you have sincerity and true confidence in your definite major purpose, you will have no trouble giving demonstrable feeling to what you are saying, and that is the essence of effective speaking.

Emotional Control

Much of what we do is directed by our feelings. Since our feelings can lift us to great achievements or hurl us down to defeat, we owe it to ourselves to understand and control them. The first step is to identify the feelings which motivate us. There are seven negative emotions and seven positive.

The seven negative emotions are:

1. Fear (discussed in the next chapter)
2. Hatred
3. Anger
4. Greed
5. Jealousy
6. Revenge
7. Superstition

The seven positive emotions are:

1. Love
2. Sex
3. Hope
4. Faith
5. Sympathy
6. Optimism
7. Loyalty

These fourteen emotions are the letters of the alphabet with which you will write your plan for success or failure. They can be combined meaningfully or chaotically.

Each emotion is related to mental attitude, and that is why I have placed so much stress on the character of one's mental attitude. These emotions are nothing but reflections of your mental attitude, which you can organize, guide, and completely command. To do so, you must take control of your mind. You must always be alert to the emotions which are present there, and embrace or reject them on the basis of their contribution to your mental attitude. Optimism will increase your confidence and flexibility; hatred will undermine your tolerance and keen sense of justice. If you do not take this control, you are condemning yourself to an entire life buffeted by the winds of emotional whim.

If you find yourself struggling to gain this control, compile a chart on which you note every day the number of times you experience and act on an emotion. Make a note of circumstances which inspire the emotions. This will give you tremendous insight into the frequency and power of your emotions. Once you know which forces trigger your emotions, you can act to eliminate them or to seek them out and use them.

Building your desire for success into a burning obsession and embarking on your definite major purpose are the cornerstones of your efforts to gain emotional control. Each strengthens the other, and progress with one will mean progress everywhere.

Alertness of Interest

You must be able to fix your interest on any person, place, or thing and hold it there for as long as the situation requires. If you cannot, the other aspects of your attractive personality will be useless. You can pay other people no greater compliment than to concentrate your attention on them when they want it. Listening well is an even greater accomplishment than speaking well.

If your interest is focused, you will gain the greatest possible advantage from any encounter. If you fidget with something in your pocket, look at your watch, or frequently glance away, you will insult the person who is speaking with you. Not only will you miss the importance of what you are being told, but the other person will instantly recognize your uninterest and begin to withdraw from the conversation.

Failure to notice the details of our own actions and of the happenings around us is an all too common weakness. Did you miss that moment of hesitation before your prospect agreed to your proposal? Recognizing it could lead you to discover some better way to offer your service. You might realize that some other service, the kind of service that your prospect would gladly renew each year on the briefest, friendliest contact, would actually be more worthwhile. Instead you might be faced with the difficult task of continually persuading someone of the dubious value of your efforts.

An alert interest in the people with whom you work is important as well. You can perceive the reasons for their success or the basis of their failures. In your mastermind group it is vital that you be aware of any changes in the situation of any contributor that might affect his or her advice.

Your memory will also be enhanced by an alert interest. If you note something clearly to begin with, it remains fixed in your mind. This is an especially practical tool in your relationship with other people. If you can recall the specifics of your conversations—even the small details of another person's life—it shows the strength of your interest in him or her. Everyone has been embarrassed by being introduced to someone for a second time, while that person shows no sign of recognition. If you show people that you remember them favorably, they will always be pleased to encounter you.

Versatility

No matter how much you know about the field of your endeavor, unless you can display a general interest in the world at large, no one is going to find you attractive. You and your associates may thrive on speaking for hours without end about the work you are doing, but you will be as unwelcome as a dentist among other people in a candy shop.

Keep yourself acquainted with the issues of the day, and maintain a few pursuits other than your business. They will broaden your character and deepen your knowledge of yourself as well. If you understand yourself, you will be better able to understand others, and they will appreciate you more for it.

Fondness for People

Just as a dog can sense those who do or do not like dogs, people recognize very quickly whether they are dealing with someone who likes other people. They resent those people with a natural dislike for their fellows, and they are attracted to those who possess genuine enthusiasm.

Even if you think you can cloak your dislike with appealing mannerisms, others will sense your lack of human affection. Guard your thoughts against uncharitable impulses, and pay particular attention to your temper. Temper is nothing but uncontrolled emotion, and when your emotions are out of control, you may suddenly say and do things which will cause you and others great injury. A person with an uncontrolled temper has a tongue that is mounted on ball bearings and swings widely and freely, with an edge as sharp as a razor blade.

Impatience with others is a visible expression of selfishness and lack of self-discipline. So, too, is a constant display of defeatism. You do no one any favors by harping on your recent misfortunes or your feelings of aimlessness. People will forgive those who aim high and miss; a person who not only lacks the get-go to make an effort but reminds others of it endlessly shows no fondness for the humor of other people. Show an alert interest, tolerance, and respect for others, and they will instinctively do the same for you.

Humility

Arrogance, vanity, and egotism are never found in someone with an attractive personality. Don't mistake humility for timidity; true humility is a recognition that even the greatest folk are, in the scheme of human existence, only fragments of the whole. Recognize that the blessings you have are a gift to be used for the common good, not topics for every conversation.

If you struggle with this issue, turn to your alert interest in others to keep you focused on topics other than yourself. As your faith grows, so will your recognition of the importance of the greater world and its value. People who are strong in faith are always humble of heart, and these qualities are always much admired.

Effective Showmanship

This is the result of the proper blend of many aspects of an attractive personality: facial expression, tone of voice, appropriate word choice, effective speech, emotional control, courtesy, versatility, mental attitude, sense of humor, and tactfulness. Together they allow you to gain favorable attention whenever necessary.

Showmanship does not imply grandstanding, clowning around, wisecracking, or gossiping. These qualities certainly grab attention, but they are tiresome and often dangerous. Effective, positive use of the traits which combine to form good showmanship will serve you well whether you are dealing with one person or a thousand.

Clean Sportsmanship

Win without boasting, lose without squealing, and others will soon respect you. Athletics can make this a habit in many people, but even if you have never set foot on a playing field or a court, you can inspire others to cooperate with you if they know that at the end of the game your presence will not be unbearable.

Your outside interests are a good place to cultivate this trait. Flexibility, tact, and humility will aid you in its display. Let your manner always be friendly, no matter what the outcome, and people will be glad to have worked with you.

A Good Handshake

This is a simple skill, really, but it is invaluable at first impression and every time a contact is renewed. Make your grasp firm and friendly, not crushing. You want to establish enthusiasm and cooperation, not competition. A limp handshake will display disdain or weakness.

Coordinate your handshake with a greeting, and grip the other person's hand for emphasis on key phrases. Maintain your grip as long as you speak your greeting in order to strengthen the impression you are making.

Be direct and assertive in your greeting, and people will associate those qualities with the whole of your personality.

Personal Magnetism

This last trait is a polite way to describe sexual energy. Of all the aspects of an attractive personality, this is the only one which is innate and cannot truly be developed by personal effort. You have what you are born with, and you cannot increase it, but you can use it.

Sexual energy is a driving, universal force. If you project it, it will aid you only if you use it properly. Proper use does not mean the physical seduction of your associates and business prospects. That way lies chaos, and such behavior is hardly consistent with other aspects of an attractive personality, such as honesty.

Rather you should channel its energy into your efforts, making them, not your body, the source of appeal to others. Use your sexual energy to build your enthusiasm, to display your genuine fondness for people, to burnish your style and tone of voice. Your gesture and posture, too, will reflect this quality.

Sexual energy is a powerful factor in an appealing personality, but it will help you only if you have refined every other trait.

Clearly all the aspects of an attractive personality rely upon and augment one another. Some—like a good handshake—can be learned quickly, others require habitual effort on your part.

Analyze your personality carefully and honestly to make sure that it embraces no displeasing traits. Even your best friends will not tell you of those aspects of your personality which may be attracting misery, opposition, and defeat. The time you devote to this analysis will pay enormous dividends, for it will not only give you a true measure of yourself but enable you to analyze and understand others.

Never make the mistake of thinking that you have done all the work you can do toward generating an attractive personality. Its standards—like its rewards—are always improving.

◆ 4 ◆

USE APPLIED FAITH

Understanding Infinite Intelligence
◆
Overcoming Disbelief
◆
Overcoming Fear
◆
Replacing Fear with Hope
◆
Demonstrating the Power of Your Faith

Faith is your awareness of, belief in, and harmonizing with the universal powers. You should not simply have faith; you must use it.

No doubt you have heard and read numerous definitions of faith, many of which involve religious convictions. For the purpose of this chapter, your own spiritual beliefs are not important, except that you will learn to put them—and much more—into daily practice.

Faith is a state of mind. For it to be useful to you in achieving lasting success, it must be an active not a passive, faith. Active faith is the process of relating yourself to the vital forces of the world, which I call Infinite Intelligence.

Understanding Infinite Intelligence

It is impossible to have active, applied faith without a positive, definite belief in a supreme being. There are many approaches to gaining such a belief. Observation, experimentation, feeling, prayer, meditation, and thought all are legitimate paths.

You learn things by seeing their effects or by accepting the statements of people you trust. In your search for knowledge about Infinite Intelligence, you may search within the external universe or within yourself.

The External World

Thinking people have always seen evidence of Infinite Intelligence in the external world. Every process of nature is orderly. The sun does not rise in the east today and the west tomorrow. Natural law endures and obtains everywhere. Such order, such continuing adherence to law, clearly implies intelligent planning and definiteness of purpose, ample evidence of Infinite Intelligence. As Tennyson wrote, "The sun, the moon, the stars, the seas, the hills and the plains./Are not these, O Soul, the Vision of Him who reigns?"

Look at the wristwatch on your arm. You know that your watch did not come into existence without the aid of organized intelligence, and you know that in this case the particular intelligence was a human one. You know equally well that this human intelligence did not originate in that single mind but that it was merely an instrument expressing the force of the natural order of the universe.

You could take that watch apart, put the pieces in a hat, and shake them about. Never in a million years would they, or could they, reassemble themselves into the smoothly functioning machine called a watch. That process requires deliberate, organized intelligence with a definite plan. Like a watch, the universe simply could not exist as it does without being the product of an Infinite Intelligence.

The Internal World

You have many senses which allow you to evaluate the external world: touch, sight, hearing, taste, smell. But you also have senses which put you in touch with another reality. The beauty of a mastermind alliance is that it puts you in touch with the creative power of others, connecting mind to mind, opening the subconscious of each member to the power of Infinite Intelligence.

Your conscience is a tool which puts you in touch with these forces. Similarly, when you engage in prayer, you explore this internal world. The power of these experiences have shaped human history again and again; the still, small voice that whispered to Saul of Tarsus changed the shape and direction of Christianity. The spiritual convictions that drove Mahatma Gandhi affected not only India but the approach to social and political changes across the globe.

This ability of the human mind to discover, embrace, and disseminate fundamental ideas and concepts is further proof of our ability to enter into a definite, positive relationship with Infinite Intelligence. You can enter this relationship and adapt it to your purposes in life. This is accomplished by applied faith.

Overcoming Disbelief

Remember, faith is a state of mind which develops by conditioning your mind to receive Infinite Intelligence. Applied faith is the adaptation of the power of Infinite Intelligence to your definite major purpose. Applied faith is the dynamo of the science of personal achievement, the source of the energy to put your thoughts into action.

In faith, you temporarily relax your own reason and willpower and open your mind completely to the inflow of Infinite Intelligence. The chapter on definiteness of purpose teaches that your mind is the only thing over which you have the right of complete control. You must control your mind so that it is regularly open to the power of Infinite Intelligence.

Whatever your mind can conceive and believe, it can achieve. Therefore, do not allow self-imposed limitations and restrictions to block the flow of Infinite Intelligence. As sunlight passing through a prism is broken up into its component rays, so Infinite Intelligence, passing through your mind, is broken up into a variety of forms. The belief that you cannot succeed, that you are not worthy, that others stand in your way, that some things cannot be done: each of these will act as an imperfection in the prism of your mind, distorting and scattering the power of Infinite Intelligence. And if you close the window of your mind to the power of Infinite Intelligence through disbelief, you will never experience its benefits.

You cannot simply announce to yourself that you have faith and expect instant results. Faith is a state of mind which must be cultivated. Set aside at least an hour a day to contemplate your relationship to Infinite Intelligence. Look for the ways in which it is manifested in your life and for places where its power can be applied.

Clear your mind of all negative thoughts of want, poverty, fear, ill health, and disharmony, and then take these three easy steps to build your faith:

1. Express a definite desire for the achievement of a purpose, and relate it to one or more of the basic human motives.

2. Create a definite and specific plan for attaining that desire.

3. Start acting on that plan, putting every conscious effort behind it.

The more you act on faith in Infinite Intelligence, the more your mind will open to its power. And the more you see that power working in your life, the easier it will be for you to act on faith. The process is a wonderful cycle.

When you face a problem or question, you can put this fledgling faith into action. Your subconscious has already been conditioned by your acting on faith to believe that you will succeed. Relax your reason so that it does not interfere with listening to the ideas, hunches, and intuitions that your subconscious conceives on the basis of this faith in your success. Look among these suggestions from your subconscious for the solution to your problem. You will recognize this solution by the soundness of the plan that occurs to you and by the feeling of enthusiasm which accompanies its recognition. As soon as you do recognize the plan, act on it at once! Do not hesitate, argue, challenge, worry, or fret about it. Act on it!

If your plan does not work out exactly as you expected, repeat this procedure. It takes time to build faith, to open your mind to its application. But remember, you cannot expect Infinite Intelligence to do your work; that's what applied faith means. If the plan you conceive through faith requires the cooperation of other people, you must work to gain it; it will not just happen. If your plan requires capital, it will not appear on your doorstep in a grocery bag; you must seek it out with the best of your abilities. You must put your faith into action.

A final word: If you make your prayers an expression of gratitude and thanksgiving for the blessings you already have, instead of requests for things you do not have, you will obtain results much faster.

Overcoming Fear

An important part of opening your mind to faith is ridding your mind of the fears which limit your belief. There are seven basic fears. Nearly everyone suffers from at least one; some of us must conquer them all. Here are the seven fears, how you can recognize their presence in your life, and how you can banish them.

The First Fear: Poverty

This is the most destructive of the seven basic fears, and the hardest to master, because it brings so much suffering and misery. Much of the fear of poverty comes from our bitter experiences in dealing with others who have proved untrustworthy and willing to exploit us for their own benefit.

If you resent poverty and are determined to be rid of it, analyze yourself fully for signs of this fear. Then fasten your mind on substitutes for the negative habits which this fear inspires.

Lack of ambition. Do you accept whatever life hands out without challenging it? Are you mentally and physically lazy? Then adopt a positive, driving ambition to vanquish this symptom of the fear of poverty.

Failure to make your own decisions. Do others determine everything that happens in your life? Do not surrender the most precious gift of your Creator! Make your own decisions and become self-determining.

Making excuses for your failures. Do you offer alibis for your lack of achievements? Do you envy and criticize the success of others? Accept that only *you* are responsible for what happens to you.

A negative mental attitude. This is the greatest limitation the fear of poverty imposes, and it can encompass all the others. Discard pessimism, expect that things will go your way, and act accordingly. Do not put things off, avoid responsibility, or live beyond your means. Instead work to make your life better, and it will be.

Developing definiteness of purpose is the first step toward replacing a negative mental attitude with a positive one. Find out what you want, and look for it all the time. Demand much! Set a high goal, believe that you will attain it with the aid of Infinite Intelligence, and you will leave the fear of poverty far behind.

The Second Fear: Criticism

Fear of criticism can affect you in ways both trivial and serious. It can lead you to buy the latest fashions, the fanciest cars, the most sophisticated stereo audio systems because you fear being left behind the times, out of step with what "everyone" is doing. More insidiously, it can prevent you from presenting and acting on ideas that are revolutionary, ideas that would give you independence. It robs you of your individuality and your faith in yourself.

Following are the most obvious symptoms of a fear of criticism and the steps you can take to eliminate them.

Keeping up with the Joneses. Trying to maintain the front of being the most current, most affluent person on the block can cripple you, both financially and emotionally. Buy what you need, and put your fiscal and mental resources to work elsewhere.

Bragging about your achievements. You do this to cover up feelings of inferiority. You imitate success rather than attain it. It's fine if your definite major purpose includes community recognition, but if you gain a false recognition, you will be constantly haunted by the prospect of exposure as a fraud. Take pride in what you have actually accomplished, and remember that there will soon come a time when your real achievements will stand for themselves.

Being easily embarrassed. This causes you to be unable to make firm decisions, to fear meeting people, and to lack self-confidence. Determine that whatever you do in pursuit of an honorable definite purpose is worthy. Remember how the neighbors laughed at Walter P. Chrysler—and how short and hollow that laughter was.

Fear of criticism is a common fear. If you let it, it will sap your initiative and imagination. But for every step you take away from it, it will take two steps away from you; once you begin your journey, it will grow easier by the day.

The Third Fear: Ill Health

This fear is closely related to a later one, the fear of death, but it is much more dependent on habits for its growth. You may very well have acquired it simply by growing up around others who shared it. It, too, can prevent you from taking risks, and its simple presence can actually bring about the very situation you so fear.

Remember that whatever your mind can conceive and believe, it can achieve. This works just as effectively in creating illness as in maintaining health. Norman Cousins effectively demonstrated the power of laughter in healing the sick— himself included. You want the power of your mind focused on maintaining your health, but certain habits demonstrate your enslavement to the fear of ill health. You must break them.

The drugstore habit. Do you run to the pharmacist every time some new cure-all is advertised? Have you consumed mountains of garlic, ginseng, and oat bran? Taking care of yourself is important, but looking to pills diverts your attention from recognizing that your own mental attitude toward your health is the most important factor in your good health.

The habit of self-pity. Do the slightest pains and discomforts keep you in bed? Is some condition your excuse for not acting? Dwell on that condition, surrender to it, and you are finished. It is an obstacle to be overcome, and it may take effort to overcome it. But every skill you develop in overcoming your condition will serve you throughout your plan for achieving success.

The habit of substance abuse. It may be drink, it may be drugs, but it's there only to cover up your fear of some mental or physical pain. You must seek out the source of that pain and address it. This process will take time, but every step of progress you make on that path will not only bring progress in overcoming your other fears but also free your time, money, and energy for achieving success.

Overcoming your fear of ill health can bring you wonderfully concrete results in so many ways. You, your family, your friends, and your ambitions will all be better off.

The Fourth Fear: Loss of Love

I knew a man once who lost everything he had—money, social position, the love of his family—when it was discovered that for years he had been cheating his business partners and evading taxes. His only explanation was that he had lavished all his ill-gotten gains upon his wife, out of fear that otherwise he would be unable to hold on to her affections.

The bitterest irony was that since he had so long focused all his efforts on the single aim of satisfying her every want, his wife had come to see him only in that light. As soon as he was no longer able to provide for her, she left him. Once she had truly loved him, but out of fear he had cultivated only one aspect of the relationship, and her affections naturally withered. What had he offered her to love but his money?

The fear of the loss of love is so intimate and so easily understood that it isn't necessary to elaborate on its symptoms. Simply cultivate your relationships with a positive mental attitude, give them your all, and instead of being a source of fear to you, they will be a bastion of strength and courage.

The Fifth Fear: Old Age

The fear of old age causes you to slow down and develop a feeling of inferiority. Whether you're thirty, forty, sixty, or seventy, you become convinced that you have let opportunity slip by and that your best years are behind you.

Nothing could be further from the truth. Every moment of

your life that has passed by has taught you invaluable lessons that you can apply today. You should have a positive appreciation for the wisdom and understanding you have gained. Most of the great achievements in human history have come from people who have blown out more than a few birthday candles.

The best way to confront this fear is to jump on it with both feet and laugh about it. Whenever you have a birthday, subtract a year from your age instead of adding one. Don't make the mistake of trying to act like a teenager, adopting the dress and speech you see on TV; that will only make you feel and look foolish. And don't ever say to yourself, "If only I were younger, I would do" something that you know you must.

There was a time when every morning as I arose, I saw Father Time sneaking up alongside me. At first I was terrified. But one day I looked him in the eye and shouted, "Get out of here, old man, and stay out! I don't need you! Get out!" Try this yourself whenever the idea occurs that you are too old to do something, and you will find that this response is quickly retrieved from your subconscious, ready to defend you whenever the fear of old age threatens.

The Sixth Fear: Loss of Liberty

No matter where you live, in any country, the fear of the loss of freedom is present. For those suffering in police states rather than enjoying the liberty that Americans possess, the fear is great. But many other forces can work to limit your freedom—the political ambitions of your neighbors, the demands of your daily life—and this fear can paralyze you and distract you from your definite major purpose.

The only way to fight this fear is to take an active role in defending the institutions that preserve your liberty. The rights we enjoy in this country were won through bitter years of struggle, and they can be maintained only by constant vigilance. You must be aware of the struggles that are taking place, you must take an active role in them, and you must also be sure that you are doing nothing that encroaches upon the liberties of others. If you become a tyrant in the pursuit of your definite major purpose, seeking to dominate your family, your mastermind alliance, and your employees, you will be rolling back the cause of freedom just as certainly as does any revolutionary extremist. You cannot be free of this fear yourself if you are not in harmony with the very forces of liberty which make your own success possible.

The Seventh Fear: Death

This fear is the grandfather of all others. It is very difficult to whip because it is so universal in our society, and because it is constantly reinforced on a daily basis.

There is no escape from death, and no matter what faiths we have, death is an unknown, for we have never experienced it. Complete, absolute answers about its nature are impossible, and it is human nature to fear anything we do not understand.

The truth is, *fear* of death can stop you in your tracks much sooner than the actual event. Overwhelmed by the possibility of the end of your existence, you may feel that action is futile and effort is meaningless. This ignores the fundamental fact that every moment of your life is valuable, that the world rolls on about you, and that your own actions can have a positive effect far beyond your own situation. Even if death comes for you in the next instant, life will not stop for those you love and those you do not even know. You have an obligation to act for the common good.

I can tell you how I have succeeded in quieting this fear. I have looked at life and death and the nature of the world. I have recognized that only two conclusions are possible: Death is either one long, eternal sleep or an experience on some plane far better than we have here on earth. Either way there is nothing to fear because it is inevitable.

Recognizing this allows you to write off the fear of death. You don't discuss it; you don't think about it. You simply realize that at one time or another you will face it, and there will be nothing you can do about it. So you accept this fact, for only a simpleminded person worries about something over which he or she has no control.

Replacing Fear with Hope

The fundamental lesson in dealing with the fear of death is learning to set it aside. This should be your goal with each of the fears, for whatever you fear will follow you around like a puppy. Your mind attracts anything it dwells upon. Most people go through life thinking about the things they don't want to happen, and they probably experience every one of them.

Wouldn't it be a better idea, then, to refuse to think about the things you don't want and to feed your mind with pictures of the things you do want? There is nothing more important than learning the art of keeping your mind focused upon the things, conditions, and circumstances you really want. This is the greatest application of applied faith you can make. When your mind has definiteness of purpose, you are in a condition to start having faith. And when you have faith, you can call upon Infinite Intelligence to apply it.

Faith exists only so long as it is used. You cannot develop muscles by not using them; you cannot increase your capital by not investing it. Persistent action backed by definiteness of purpose will pump up your faith.

Demonstrating the Power of Your Faith

The key to putting your faith into action is to have a positive mental attitude. Here are steps to build your faith and your PMA.

Step one. Adopt a definite major purpose, and begin to attain it. Follow the instructions in the first chapter. Know what you want, and get busy creating it. Be sure that the object of your desire is something worthy, something you can obtain. Never sell yourself short, but do not set a task for yourself which is utterly ridiculous.

Step two. Affirm the object of your desire through prayer, morning and night. Inspire your imagination to see yourself already in possession of it. When you attain one goal, set a new one. Do not let complacency set in. Bill Gates founded Microsoft, the software company that supplies the operating systems for more than 70 percent of the computers in the world. By the time he was thirty-five, his company was bigger than McDonald's, Disney, and CBS. Did he stop there?

No, he continued to dream of new roles for himself and his corporation. By the time he was thirty-seven, he had embarked on a new path to provide systems to link every machine in an office: telephone, fax machines, computers, all working together seamlessly. And he managed to bind such giants as AT&T and IBM to his vision, enlisting them in a consortium to develop and deliver that magnificent system.

You will achieve precisely the success you can envision for yourself. Cultivate that vision every day, in every way you can.

Step three. Associate as many as possible of the ten basic human motives mentioned on page 18 with your definite major purpose. Give yourself a compelling motive for doing what you want to do. Then renew that motive by bringing it up in your mind as often as possible on a daily basis. If your motives include a fine home, a nice car, and a good wardrobe, visualize those things around you. Go through the motions of driving that car or wandering about that house. Do not hesitate to use your imagination to fuel your burning desire.

Step four. Write out a list of all the advantages of your definite major purpose, and call them into your mind as often as you can. This will make you success-conscious by the power of self-suggestion. It will steady your resolve when things do not appear to be going well. If you're caught in an impossible job, you can keep yourself smiling by thinking of what you'll be doing once you're free.

Step five. Associate with people who are in sympathy with you and your major purpose; get their encouragement. They can be colleagues, friends, or family. One realtor I know occasionally comes home discouraged, but she has an agreement with her husband that covers this circumstance. The instant she lets go a defeatist sigh, he pulls out her certificate from the Million Dollar Club and a list of previous sales she's made. "Whose name do you see here? Who sold all those houses? Who sold that place down by the lake that had been on the market two years? Who saw what a dream house it could be? Isn't this latest offering just as good?"

That's all it takes, and she's out the door or on the phone again. And her husband? Don't think that he isn't inspired by his wife's determination, that his own work isn't better after he's seen what a little encouragement can do. We all need people to give us a boost, and we all benefit from doing the same for others.

Step six. Don't let a day pass without making at least one definite move toward attaining your major purpose. Keep up that persistent action. That realtor may not sell a house every day, but you can be sure that she's showing it, that she's talking it up, that she's reviewing her list of clients, that she's walking through it by herself, imagining what a wonderful home it will make for a family. Each of these steps may not be the actual sale, but they're as much as part of it as the actual closing.

Step seven. Choose a "pacesetter." Pick someone prosperous, self-reliant, and successful, and make up your mind not only to catch up with that person but to pass him or her by. Don't tell anyone this is your goal. The point is not to win a public contest but to get where you want to go.

Step eight. Surround yourself with books, pictures, mottoes, and other suggestive devices. Pick things that symbolize and reinforce achievement and self-reliance. Work constantly to add to your collection, to move things to new places, where you can see them in a different light and in association with different things. My realtor friend kept a framed copy of her Million Dollar Club certificate over her desk. One day she took it down to dust and set it on top of a newspaper. When she picked it up again, she saw beneath it an article about the new football coach who had been hired at the university. He would need a place to live! Guess who bought that house she'd been struggling to sell?

As you build an atmosphere of support, keep a notebook handy to jot down the things you hear and read that inspire you. When you're on the road or in a meeting, your fast scratchings can give you lasting support.

Step nine. Never run away from disagreeable circumstances. Fight them, with all your resources, right where you stand and without a moment's delay.

This doesn't mean taking a swing at the fellow who tells you no. It does mean not accepting that refusal and bringing every faculty you have to bear on changing that person's mind. Or you may have to take a hard look at yourself, find the error you made, and resolve then and there to correct it. Sometimes adverse circumstances are testing devices, providing means by which you may be promoted from a given task to a greater one.

Remember, you are what you are and where you are because of the dominating thoughts in your mind. Procrastination in dealing with these thoughts only sentences you to further limitation and frustration.

Step ten. Recognize that anything worth having has a definite price tag. Anything worth having is worth working for. The price of self-reliance is eternal vigilance in applying your faith.

Close the door of fear behind you, and you will quickly see the door of faith open before you. Increasing and applying your faith are a process that takes time and dedication. You will never be finished with this task because the power you have at your disposal is infinite. So are the rewards.

◆ 5 ◆

GO THE EXTRA MILE

Thomas Edison's Only Partner
◆
The Nordstrom Phenomenon
◆
My Own Journey
◆
The Benefits of Doing More than You Are Paid For
◆
The Extra Mile Formula

Render more and better service than you are paid for, and sooner or later you will receive compound interest from your investment. It is inevitable that every seed of useful service you sow will sprout and reward you with an abundant harvest.

Going the extra mile is not the sort of principle that can be put into practice in a few easy steps. Instead it is a state of mind that you must develop, so that it is a part of everything you do. There is a subtle, but powerful, mental attitude connected with it. The stories that follow will demonstrate that attitude and show you the concrete benefits it brings.

Remember, your best recommendation is the one you give yourself by rendering superior service in the right mental attitude.

Thomas Edison's Only Partner

Edward C. Barnes was a man of much determination but few resources. He was determined to ally himself with the greatest mind of his day, Thomas Edison. When he arrived in Edison's office unannounced, his poor appearance made the clerks laugh, especially when he revealed that he had come to be Mr. Edison's partner. Edison had never had a partner. But his persistence got him an interview with Edison, and that interview got him a job as a handyman.

Edison was impressed with Barnes's determination, but that alone was insufficient to convince him to take the extraordinary step of making him a partner. Instead Barnes spent years cleaning and repairing equipment, until one day he heard Edison's sales force laughing over the latest invention, the dictaphone.

They said it would never sell. Why replace a secretary with a machine? But Barnes, the handyman, jumped up and cried, "I can sell it!" He got the job.

For a month Barnes pounded the New York City pavement on a handyman's salary. At the end of that month he had sold seven machines. When he returned to Edison, full of ideas for selling more machines all across the country, Edison made him his partner in the dictaphone business, the only partner Edison ever had.

What made Barnes so important to Edison? The inventor had thousands of people working for him, but only Barnes was willing to display his faith in Edison's work and to put that faith into action. He didn't demand a fancy expense account and a big salary to do it either.

Barnes focused favorable attention on himself by rendering service far beyond a handyman's responsibility. As the only one of Edison's employees to render this service, he was the only one who uncovered such tremendous benefits for himself.

The Nordstrom Phenomenon

Starting out in a simple shoe store in the 1920s in Seattle, the Nordstrom family has built a chain of department stores famous around the country for service and willingness to bend over backward to please their customers.

A garment may be returned anytime it fails to satisfy, even years after the original purchase. Sales associates will call branches all across the country to find an item in the size and color a customer wants. One woman even sent a Mother's Day card on behalf of a customer who mentioned that she had forgotten to do so.

Store executives acknowledge that a policy of such dedication to the customer leaves them open to abuse. People buy clothes to wear once and then return them. Items are special-ordered and never picked up. A few folk seem to regard Nordstrom sales associates as their personal gofers. It doesn't matter. By delivering service that is so far and above that of any department store in the country, Nordstrom has developed tremendous customer loyalty. In an economic climate that saw giants like Macy's, Bloomingdale's, Marshall Field, Sears, and J. C. Penney closing stores or laying off employees, Nordstrom continued a slow and steady expansion coast to coast, never opening a new store until it was sure it had assembled a crew of employees dedicated to its own brand of going-the-extra-mile service.

My Own Journey

I accepted Andrew Carnegie's commission to organize and publish the principles of success when I was a law student at Georgetown University. Other than reimbursement for some traveling expenses, I got no compensation from Carnegie for my efforts.

My dedication to my task placed strains on my life. I had a family to support, and many of my relatives ridiculed me for my goal. In spite of this opposition, I worked for twenty years, interviewing presidents, inventors, founders of great companies, and famous philanthropists. Because these people were often unaware of the principles they employed—they just *did* it—it took a great deal of time for me to observe them and determine whether the forces I supposed were operating actually were. Instead of making money for myself, I had a job to do for others.

Believe me, there were times when, between the needling of my relatives and the hardships I endured, it was not easy to maintain a positive mental attitude and persevere. Sometimes, in barren hotel rooms, I almost believed my family was right. The thing that kept me going was my conviction that one day I would not only successfully complete my work but also be proud of myself when it was finished.

Sometimes, when the flames of hope dwindled to a flicker, I had to fan them with everything I possessed to keep them from going out. It was my faith in Infinite Intelligence that tided me over these rough spots and saw me through.

Did it pay to go the extra mile for twenty years and endure all those hardships? The answer is obvious.

The Benefits of Doing More than You Are Paid For

Since going the extra mile can involve hardship, it will help you to be conscious of all the different benefits it will bring.

The Law of Increasing Returns

The quantity and quality of the extra service you render will come back to you greatly multiplied. Consider the farmer who plants a crop of wheat. If he harvested only one grain of wheat for each grain he planted, he'd be wasting his time. Instead every successful grain produces a stalk and a sheaf containing many more grains. Of course, a few don't sprout, but whatever problems a farmer may face, getting back many times more wheat grains than he or she planted isn't one of them.

And so it is with everything you do in the service you render. If you render service worth a hundred dollars, chances are you will get back not only that one hundred dollars but perhaps ten times that—provided you have done so with the right mental attitude.

If you render extra service unwillingly or resentfully, you will probably get nothing back. It's as if the farmer had sown his wheat on the interstate road instead of the fertile field. And if you render your service only with a sharp eye out for your own benefit, you will get nothing except perhaps a poke in that eye.

One rainy afternoon an elderly lady walked into a Philadelphia department store. Most of the clerks ignored her, but one solicitous young man asked if he could help her. When she replied that she was just waiting for the rain to end, he didn't try to sell her something she didn't want, and he didn't turn his back. Instead he brought her a chair.

When the rain let up, the lady thanked the young man and asked for his card. A few months passed, and the owner of the store received a letter asking that this young man be sent to Scotland to take orders for furnishing an entire castle! The letter writer was the elderly lady for whom the clerk had provided a chair. She also happened to be Andrew Carnegie's mother.

By the time the young clerk had his bags packed for Scotland, he was a partner in that department store. This was the result of the Law of Increasing Returns, all because he had shown a little concern and courtesy when no one else would.

The Law of Compensation

The Law of Compensation ensures that everything you do will bring you some sort of result of the same kind. To benefit from this, you must always render the most service you are capable of, with the best attitude, and you must do so regardless of your immediate compensation, even if it appears you will receive no immediate compensation.

The issue here is not some unlooked-for benefit, such as might come from offering a chair to a senior citizen. It is a matter of honesty and earnest effort. Dishonest, lazy people look to get something for less than is required—or even nothing. If you decide to boost your profits by raising your rates and providing less service, it's going to catch up with you.

AT&T learned this lesson the hard way. Its rates continued to climb, and it did nothing to offer its customers any new advantages. Along came deregulation, MCI, and Sprint, and bang! Customers began switching their long-distance service by the hundreds of thousands. AT&T saw its error quickly, though, cut its rates, and began offering innovative packages. It still faces heavy competition, but it now knows quite a bit about the Law of Compensation.

In contrast, consider mobile home builder Jim Clayton. His company, Clayton Homes, was already growing rapidly when Hurricane Andrew decimated South Florida. The need for new mobile homes was enormous and fast. Clayton could have followed the examples of many Florida business owners and jacked his prices skyward. Instead Clayton Homes kept its prices level and jacked its production skyward. The Law of Compensation meant that the company still made a reasonable profit on its services; it also means that thousands of home buyers in South Florida have reason to remember Clayton Homes very fondly when it comes to their next purchase.

Your day-to-day life may not offer such dramatic examples, but the most concrete one is your paycheck. If you are dissatisfied with its size, remember: Until you begin to render more service than you are already being paid for, you are not entitled to any more pay.

If you are convinced that you are already doing more

work than you are being paid for, ask yourself why the Law of Compensation doesn't seem to be working.

The sad fact is that most people have no definite purpose greater than getting that paycheck. No matter how hard they work, the wheel of fortune turns right past them because they neither expect nor demand more.

What are you doing that shows you expect and demand more than what you currently get?

Gaining Favorable Attention

People who need your work have things to offer you. You probably are not the only person capable of providing what they need. What will distinguish you from the crowd? The attention you generate by doing more than you are being paid to do.

Early one morning Charles Schwab arrived at one of the steel mills he managed. There, in the dawn's faint light, was a clerk from the company's stenography pool. When Schwab wondered what he was doing there, the man explained that he had come in case there were any letters or telegrams Schwab wanted sent right away. It would be hours before the rest of the staff arrived.

Schwab thanked the fellow and told him he might need him later that day. And he did. That night, as Schwab headed back to the main office, he took along his new personal assistant, the fellow who had gotten his attention so early in the morning.

It wasn't the fact that this young man was an extraordinary stenographer that got him attention. It was his habit of showing his personal initiative in going the extra mile.

Becoming Indispensable

Whether you are an employee or the head of your own company, going the extra mile makes you indispensable to others. You do for them what no one else does. There may be others with more knowledge, skill, or prestige, but you are the only one who provides something absolutely necessary. There may be seven other companies providing public relations expertise, but if you are the one who can be called upon at two in the morning with a can-do attitude when a disaster strikes, people will remember and value that.

One young man, working for a movie talent agency, was the only person willing to listen to a cantankerous star complain about her problems hour after hour, day after day. No one else took the time. When she threw a tantrum on the set one day, he, not the director, the producer, the heads of the studio, or her agent, was the only one to persuade her to go back to work. The movie went back on schedule, and millions of dollars were saved. He had made himself indispensable by befriending that important client.

You will never command more than average compensation until you become indispensable to somebody or some group. Make yourself so useful that it would be extremely difficult, if not impossible, to replace you. People who have pulled themselves out of the crowd and have included the priceless ingredients of going the extra mile and personal initiative in their service virtually write their own paychecks.

Self-Improvement

Going the extra mile means that you strengthen your ability to do your job and to do it well. Carrying out your tasks in a state of mind focused on providing the best service possible in the best possible attitude reinforces your skills. By imposing systematic self-discipline, you understand the process better every time, and you impress upon your subconscious the need for quality work. Remember the adage: "Strength and struggle go hand in hand."

You should never make a presentation, design a software program, or do anything at all connected with your definite major purpose without the deliberate intention of doing it better than you have ever done it before. True, you may sometimes fail or not meet your previous standards, but the very intention of surpassing your previous best is a healthy habit that will ultimately cause you to excel.

Doing a job just to get it done, complaining about the tasks before you, and grumbling about your pay are not ways to make yourself excel. Always stay focused on doing your best possible work.

Opportunity

When you have made yourself indispensable, you will gain not only security in the job you have but the ability to select the work that you do. Perhaps this will mean a promotion, a job at another company, or your choice of clients. Going the extra mile is a way of writing yourself an insurance policy against the fear of poverty, against the fear of want, and against competition from those who only go halfway.

Consider William Novak. After years of rewarding but not particularly lucrative work as a writer, he was hired to be the coauthor of Chrysler CEO Lee Iacocca's autobiography. Working with the fascinating details of Iacocca's life, Novak wrote an utterly compelling book that was a national bestseller for well over a year. Iacocca's life story probably would have made a successful book without much effort, but Novak delivered something so readable and inspiring that the book became a phenomenon.

Now Novak's name as cowriter on any project opens every door in the publishing world and commands advances much higher than those written by other people. He can choose his subjects, and he can pick from among the best. By going the extra mile, he made certain that he would always have the work he wanted.

Favorable Contrast

Going the extra mile turns a spotlight on you and gives you the important benefit of favorable contrast with others.

An inspired window designer at Marshall Field's once filled a display with handsome ties. In the center was a full-length mirror. Businessmen who stopped to look at the display admired the ties and then saw themselves in the mirror. By contrast, their ties looked dull and shabby. Many were tempted to go in and pick up a snappy new tie which looked so much better than their own. That's the power of contrast.

People are always making comparisons, and we notice the things that are different. If you render more and better service than others, you will naturally stand out in bold contrast.

Wise employers are very alert to the power of contrast, and they reward the employees it highlights. Some do decide to ignore that contrast and reap the benefits of extra service from their workers without compensating their workers. But the spotlight of contrast is bright enough that their competitors will sooner or later see the person standing in it. There are so few people who step into this spotlight that if it shines on you, others will notice soon.

Pleasing Attitude

When you do more than you are immediately paid to do in a willing and cheerful manner, you develop a positive, pleasing attitude, the cornerstone of an attractive personality.

When you have an attractive personality, you can get almost anyone to behave toward you exactly as you wish. That's something worthwhile, isn't it? Treat other people precisely as you wish them to treat you; apply the Golden Rule. If they don't respond at once, keep at it, again and again and again. If it never works, then you need to decide whether you want to keep working with these people. It may be time to fire your employer.

Personal Initiative

Personal initiative means doing what needs to be done without being told. It is the most outstanding trait of the American personality, yet sadly it is a quality missing in many people. Going the extra mile develops personal initiative because you don't wait for things to happen but make them happen.

When your mind is always focused on doing the best job possible, you are forced to look at every situation thoroughly. No doubt something will have to be done that is out of the ordinary. Part of your service is getting this thing accomplished, and that means putting personal initiative to work.

There are people who go through life rendering extra service yet wind up in the poorhouse. They are honest and dependable, adjectives for traits that give others the chance to cheat and exploit them, and they never do a thing about it because they lack personal initiative.

It's one thing to cast your bread upon the waters; it's another to pretend not to notice when it just comes back wet and soggy. You must use personal initiative to see that your efforts are expended in the right areas. Investigate to make sure that the people you work for are honest and trustworthy, that they aren't about to go belly-up and be unable to pay you. And if you find yourself deceived, find yourself someone else to work for. Personal initiative is not simply for the benefit of others.

Self-Confidence

Going the extra mile builds your conviction that you are doing what is good and right. It puts you on better terms with your conscience, and it gives you faith in yourself.

Sometimes the hardest person to get along with is the one who uses your toothbrush, the same one you see in the mirror every morning. Talk to that person; explain your plans and purposes; seek cooperation. Outline your strategy for rendering extra service, and listen to the answer you get. If it's doubtful, you need to spend a little more time selling yourself.

A man who was ragged and downcast came to see me once. I recognized his name as that of a once-prominent restaurant owner who had recently lost everything when his partner went bankrupt. He wanted my help.

I asked him to stand in front of a pair of drapes, and I told him that in just a moment I was going to introduce him to the only person in the world who could help him regain his self-confidence and overcome defeat. Then I yanked the drapes open to reveal a full-length mirror.

He stared at the mirror for a few minutes, speechless, and then left my office with thanks. Months passed before he strode into my office completely renewed. His thanks now were effusive. He had reminded himself of his skill in business, found new backers similarly convinced of his abilities, and was currently running one of the most popular spots in Chicago.

When you build your self-confidence through the knowledge that you are giving the best possible service, you develop the reserves of determination to see you through dramatic setbacks without the kinds of theatrics I had to employ with this fellow. Trust yourself, and you will always have someone to rely on.

Overcoming Procrastination

When you are doing your work eagerly and cheerfully, you avoid the temptation to do it this afternoon instead, or maybe tomorrow. In fact, you probably won't be able to wait to get started. Have you ever wondered at the stories about famous people who get up at some seemingly ungodly hour to begin their work? They do it because they're eager to do what they are doing, and they have gained their fame because of that eagerness.

When you act as soon as you must, the habit of procrastination dies from not being fed, and no one laments its passing.

The Extra Mile Formula

To help you keep your mind fixed on going the extra mile, I have developed the following formula, the only one in this book. It's very simple: $Q^1 + Q^2 + MA = C$.

Q^1 is the *quality* of service rendered.
Q^2 is the *quantity* of service rendered.
MA is the *mental* attitude in which it is rendered.
C is your *compensation*.

"Compensation" here means all the things that come into your life: money, joy, harmony with others, spiritual enlightenment, faith, an open mind, a sense of tolerance, or anything else worthwhile that you seek.

Always be aware of the diverse nature of compensation. Money is nice, but it certainly will not be the only thing that makes you successful—or allows you to enjoy success. Do not cut off relationships which are poor in financial rewards but rich in other qualities, for no matter how much service you render, others will recognize your one-sided approach. The spotlight of contrast will shine on you unfavorably then and will seek out those who remain true to the spirit of going the extra mile.

♦ 6 ♦
CREATE PERSONAL
INITIATIVE

The Major Attributes of Personal Initiative
♦
Personal Initiative Is Contagious
♦
Personal Initiative Succeeds Where Others Fail
♦
Personal Initiative Creates Work
♦
Personal Initiative Creates Opportunity
♦
Personal Initiative Creates the Future
♦
Personal Initiative Creates Advancement
♦
Putting Personal Initiative to Work

One of the biggest benefits from going the extra mile is the emphasis it requires you to place on personal initiative. This chapter will round out your understanding of personal initiative, and through example it will show you how to multiply that quality in yourself.

Andrew Carnegie once told me, "There are two types of people who never amount to anything. There are those who never do anything except what they are told to do. And there are those who cannot even do what they are told to do. The people who get ahead do the things that should be done without being told. And they don't stop there. They go the extra mile and do much more than is expected of them."

Personal initiative is absolutely necessary if you are going to realize your goal. It will bring you advancement, attention, and opportunity.

The Major Attributes of Personal Initiative

In the years I spent formulating these principles of success, I observed many extraordinary people. What follows is a list of qualities that constantly appeared in my observations. Some of them will be things that have already been covered in this book; others come later. The important thing for you to do here is to identify these characteristics in yourself as you are now and to think about how you can increase and strengthen them.

- The adoption of a definite major purpose
- The motivation to act continuously in pursuit of that purpose
- A mastermind alliance to acquire the power to attain that purpose
- Self-reliance
- Self-discipline
- Persistence, based upon the will to win
- Well-developed imagination, controlled and directed
- The habit of prompt, definite decision making
- The habit of basing opinions on known facts, not guesswork
- The habit of going the extra mile
- The capacity to generate enthusiasm at will and control it
- A well-developed sense of details
- The capacity to listen to criticism without resentment
- Familiarity with the ten basic human motives

- The capacity to concentrate attention on one task at a time
- Assuming full responsibility for one's own actions
- Willingness to accept full responsibility for the mistakes of subordinates
- Patience with subordinates and associates
- Recognizing the merits and abilities of others
- A positive mental attitude at all times
- The capacity for applied faith
- The habit of following through
- The habit of emphasizing thoroughness instead of speed
- Dependability

No doubt many of these qualities are already familiar to you. You may think, "I've already got that." But it is the nature of the Seventeen Principles of Success that each depends upon the others, and you can't develop one without relying upon and developing others at the same time. How can you develop faith without applying it through personal initiative? And how can you have personal initiative without a definite purpose to carry out? You can't.

Personal Initiative Is Contagious

During the Second World War Henry Kaiser astounded the world by the speed and efficiency of his shipbuilding. What made his achievement so remarkable is that he hadn't been a shipbuilder before he responded to the needs of the war. The quality that made this possible was his personal initiative, and the most obvious manifestation of this quality was his habit of following through.

When Kaiser ordered a trainload of steel to be delivered at his shipyards on a given date, he made sure that the railroad was alerted, that his own workers were prepared to accept the shipment, and, first of all, that the steel was being produced on schedule. He sent an expediter to the steel mill to keep him informed of progress and then to travel with the shipment to see that it wasn't sidetracked or delayed.

Because Kaiser was so attentive to the details of his operation, everyone who worked for him knew that the same quality was expected of themselves. If something went wrong along the way, the expediter was expected to do whatever was necessary to correct the problem and make up for lost time. And he seldom failed!

Kaiser's persistent personal initiative was an example to thousands of people on a daily basis.

Personal Initiative Succeeds Where Others Fail

Not long after I married, I paid my first visit to my wife's family. The train took me close to her hometown but stopped two miles away. Since I arrived in a downpour, by the time I reached my in-laws' house, I was not an impressive sight. I was also in something of a bad temper, and I exclaimed, "Why don't you have the railroad build a line into town?"

My brothers-in-law laughed and told me that they had been trying for ten years but that the railroad was unwilling to take on the expense of building a bridge across the local river.

"Ten years!" I said arrogantly. "Why, I could do that job in three months."

Well, I had really put my foot in it, for a boast like that in front of my new family was a challenge to them. I knew I had to act. My brothers-in-law and I waited for the rain to stop, then headed down to the river.

There we saw a creaky old wooden bridge, across which ran the county road. A freight railroad terminated at the far side of the river, its tracks crossing the road. As the freight trains came and went, they halted traffic on the road, slowing travel for all the local people.

And there was my idea. "Look," I said. "It's simple. The

passenger railroad pays for a third of the cost of a bridge so that it can offer better service to the town. The county pays for a third of the bridge because it will need to replace that wooden one soon anyway. And the freight railroad pays the final third so it gets the traffic off its tracks and prevents the inevitable accident from having all those people lined up waiting to cross."

It was that simple. In a week my brothers-in-law and I had all three parties agreed to the plan, and in three months the new bridge was up and the town had passenger rail service.

Now, I hope that your personal initiative won't have to get you out of the kind of trap I set for myself. But if you apply it at every opportunity—especially after you have made a foolish mistake—then it will benefit both you and your community.

Personal Initiative Creates Work

I once knew a rather plain fellow who didn't seem suited for much. He had been apprenticed to a plumber, but because he showed no real aptitude for plumbing, his boss tried him out as a sales rep. He didn't show an aptitude there either.

Since his handwriting was neat, the boss made him a bookkeeper next. Again, the results were discouraging.

But the bookkeeping experience taught him something: the importance of accurate inventory. So he sat down to take an inventory of himself. He decided he had these positive qualities:

1. The habit of saving money
2. The ability to figure accurately the costs of a plumbing job
3. The ability to recognize superior skills in others that he lacked himself
4. Persistence
5. The ability to induce others to work in harmony

What could he do with these skills? The answer was obvious. He set out to open his own plumbing business. He found a location, sought out the best workers he could find, and began to pursue contracts. Within a year his schedule was filled, and because he was able to bring his work in at the projected costs and to do it with quality labor, he quickly gained a reputation as the best plumber for the job—even though he was a poor plumber himself!

It was only by acting on personal initiative that this man was able to make anything of his life. Starting with a definite major purpose, step by step he built a mastermind alliance of skilled employees, delivered extra service, and attained success. If he hadn't struck out on his own, his former boss would have soon thrown up his hands and fired him. This fellow created a job for himself!

Personal Initiative Creates Opportunity

Neil Balter was a carpenter's apprentice making just four hundred dollars a week when he was hired to build some shelves in a closet. By the time he was finished and saw how grateful his client was to have better use of his space and how happy he was with the quality of his work, Balter had an idea. With money from that first satisfied customer, Balter started the California Closet Company.

The incredible transformation of a crowded closet into efficient space was such a popular idea that within twelve years Balter had more than a hundred franchises around the country. Other entrepreneurs were so impressed with his idea that copycat companies sprang up across the nation. And in 1989 Balter sold his company for twelve million dollars to Williams-Sonoma.

Neil Balter could have been content just learning to be a carpenter. But he identified his skills, set himself a definite goal, and succeeded beyond the wildest dreams of any apprentice.

Personal Initiative Creates the Future

Herbert Bass and Alex Geisler were doing production work at a Philadelphia television station in the 1960s. They saw that videotape had much more flexibility for the television market than film did. Even though they were not considered top production experts, they decided to strike out on their own.

They created Unitel Video. Because they couldn't offer production expertise that would stand out in the market, they chose to provide something else just as valuable: They offered the best in equipment and space to other production companies. Even though they were getting in on the business early, they still faced competition; to build their share of the market, they took on clients who couldn't work anywhere else because nobody thought they could pay their bills.

Bass and Geisler also knew the importance of going the extra mile. They knew that their clients had their own clients to keep happy. By offering the latest technology, they offered their clients an advantage. As Geisler told *Success* magazine, "We show our client techniques he wouldn't have thought of. He gets the credit. We get paid."

Besides doing production work for shows like *The Simpsons* and *Star Trek: The Next Generation,* Unitel now provides training seminars for video technicians around the country. It also offers corporate communications services for companies like IBM and Citibank, putting together video conferences that can link people in New York, Los Angeles, San Antonio, and Minneapolis just as if they were in the same room.

Bass and Geisler weren't the first to see that video had a place in the future. But because they had the initiative to go after what they saw, to make a plan, to take risks, to offer things that no one else was offering, their company is now first in its field.

Personal Initiative Creates Advancement

Your definite goal may someday include being your own boss, but if it doesn't, or even if that step is still some ways off, personal initiative can still pay off for you.

Amy Hilliard-Jones was a marketing strategist at Gillette. She saw an opportunity in a product Gillette had dropped as unsuccessful: White Rain shampoo. White Rain was an inexpensive, no-frills shampoo. It didn't offer anything fancy, but it should have an appeal for cost-conscious consumers. She developed a campaign to relaunch White Rain, presented it to executives, and persuaded them of its value. They went for it, and White Rain became one of Gillette's top-selling shampoos.

That made Hilliard-Jones an obvious candidate for revitalizing the Lustrasilk Corporation, a newly acquired Gillette subsidiary targeting the ethnic hair care market. She created a whole new product line, Moisture Max, which was phenomenally successful.

Today Hilliard-Jones is executive vice-president of the Burrell Communications Group, which specializes in marketing services directed at African Americans for Fortune 500 companies. She got where she is because she consistently used her personal initiative to bring bigger and better things to the companies that employed her. Those companies recognized her dedication to offering service above and beyond what was expected. So did the Harvard Business School, which gave her the Max and Cohen Award for Excellence in Retailing, and *Dollars & Sense* magazine, which named her one of the "Top 100 Business and Professional Women." Personal initiative paid off for Amy Hilliard-Jones in recognition, advancement, and the opportunity to do exactly what she wanted.

Putting Personal Initiative to Work

The time to begin exercising your personal initiative is the moment you decide upon your major purpose. Begin creating your plan of action; start assembling your mastermind alliance. You may find that your purpose changes as a result of things you learn in accomplishing these tasks, but the important thing is to begin work immediately.

It is better to act on a plan that is still weak than to delay acting at all. Procrastination is the archenemy of personal initiative, and if you let it become a habit this early in the game, it will plague your every move.

Do the best job you can putting your plan into action, and learn from your mistakes. Ignore the doomsayers who tell you that you are heading for disaster. When Andrew Carnegie went into the steel business with the goal of dropping the price of steel from $140 a ton to $20 a ton, there were plenty who scoffed. None of those people made a penny when Carnegie achieved his goal.

If you need advice, seek out skilled experts, and pay them for their counsel. The "free advice" you will get on every hand from colleagues and "friends" will be worth exactly what it costs you: nothing.

Never wait for some outside force to trigger your actions. Of course, you will have to respond to surprises and your competition, but you must be moving forward according to your own plan on a daily basis. Feed your burning desire with images of your successful self. Stoke its flames so high that they burn your seat, so that you won't be able to sit back in your chair and take it easy when you ought to be following up on your work of the day before.

When a task is completed, examine it. Is it the best job you could have done? What might have made it better? Why don't you take that step right now? Personal initiative depends on your being alert to every opportunity and acting on that opportunity as soon as you discover it.

◆ ◆ ◆

Clearly, personal initiative is a demanding quality, and its practice requires a good deal of mental resources. When your initiative is flagging, you can turn to the principle which breathes life into and restores every one of the others: positive mental attitude.

✦ 7 ✦

BUILD A POSITIVE MENTAL ATTITUDE

The Choice of Two Envelopes
✦
The Rewards of a Positive Mental Attitude
✦
The Penalties of a Negative Mental Attitude
✦
How to Develop a Positive Mental Attitude
✦
The 2 Percent Who Succeed
✦
Join the 2 Percent Club

A positive mental attitude is the single most important principle of the science of success. You will depend upon it in everything you do. You cannot get the maximum benefit out of the other sixteen principles without understanding and employing PMA.

The Choice of Two Envelopes

At birth you arrive figuratively clutching two sealed envelopes. One is labeled "Rewards," and the other "Penalties." The first envelope contains a list of all the benefits you will enjoy from taking possession of your own mind and using it to get what you want. The second carries a list of the consequences that will befall you if you neglect controlling your mind and directing it toward a worthwhile goal.

Read that paragraph again. Now read it once more. Its message is that important.

This chapter will open those envelopes for you and reveal their specific contents. You will see that these envelopes are real, that the rewards and penalties they contain are real.

Nature abhors two things: a vacuum and idleness. If you do not use a muscle, it will wither and become useless. If you do not use the powers of your mind, they will do the same thing. Your brain and your life will become subject to every passing influence, unable to resist them or to act positively—unless you fix your mind on the object of your desire and create and act upon a plan for attaining it.

You've probably heard something like the old saying "Success attracts success while failure attracts more failure." Nothing could be more true. Striving for success makes you better able to attain it. Doing nothing and accepting failure only bring more failure your way.

If you put your mind to work with a positive mental attitude and believe that success is your right, your belief will guide you unerringly toward whatever your definition of success might be. If you adopt a negative mental attitude and fill your mind with thoughts of fear and frustration, your mind will only draw those same things to you.

That is the power of mental attitude. Why not make yours positive?

The Rewards of a Positive Mental Attitude

If you take possession of your mind and direct it toward desirable goals, you will enjoy:

1. Success consciousness, which attracts only the circumstances which make for success
2. Sound health, both physical and mental
3. Financial independence
4. A labor of love in which to express yourself
5. Peace of mind
6. Applied faith, which makes fear impossible
7. Enduring friendships
8. Longevity and a well-balanced life
9. Immunity from self-limitation
10. The wisdom to understand yourself and others

The Penalties of a Negative Mental Attitude

If you neglect taking possession of your mind and directing it toward a worthwhile goal, you are doomed to:

1. Poverty and misery your entire life
2. Mental and physical ailments of all kinds
3. Self-limitations which trap you in mediocrity
4. Fear and all its destructive consequences
5. Hatred of the means by which you support yourself
6. Many enemies and few friends
7. Every brand of worry known to humanity
8. Being a victim of every negative influence you encounter
9. Subjection to the will of others
10. A wasted life which does nothing to better the human condition

Which choice will you make? If you do not make the first one and embrace it wholeheartedly, the second will be forced on you. There is no halfway point, no compromise. Which choice will you make?

How to Develop a Positive Mental Attitude

You must have a positive mental attitude to make life pay off on your own terms. Nothing great has ever been achieved without PMA.

Recognize that your mental attitude is the only thing over which you—and only you—have complete control. Exercise that control, and direct it by using PMA.

Realize, and prove to your own satisfaction by making it so, that every adversity, sorrow, or defeat, whether or not you caused it to happen, contains the seed of an equivalent benefit which you can nurture into a blessing that soars above the disaster that brought it.

Learn to close the door of your mind on all failures from your past. Clear your mind of any influence which does not support a positive mental attitude.

Find out what you want most in life, and go after it. Do it right now by helping others to acquire similar benefits. This way you put the principle of going the extra mile into action.

Select the person who, in your opinion, is the finest person in all the world, past or present. Make him or her your pacesetter for the rest of your life, emulating him or her in every possible way.

Determine what kind of resources you need, set up a plan for acquiring them based on the idea of not too much, not too little. Don't think small, but remember, greed more than anything else has destroyed ambitious people.

Form the habit of saying or doing something every day which will make someone else feel better. You can do this with a phone call, a postcard, or a simple act of kindness. Give someone a good inspirational book, for instance, and you give that person something that will work wonders in his or her life. One good deed a day will keep old man gloom away.

Make yourself understand that what whips you isn't defeat, but your mental attitude toward it. Train yourself to look for the seed of equivalent benefit in every disappointment you face.

Ascertain what you like best to do, and do it as a labor of love with your heart and soul. Perhaps it will simply be a hobby. That's fine. Just remember that an idle mind quickly becomes a negative mind; it's called brooding.

Understand that often when you have searched in vain for a solution to a problem, you can find it by helping someone else solve his or her problem. By the time you have solved the other person's problem, you will have the insight to solve your own.

Study Ralph Waldo Emerson's "Essay on Compensation" once a week until you understand and have assimilated it. This powerful work will convince you of the benefits you will derive from PMA.

Take a complete inventory of every asset you possess. You will discover that your greatest asset is a sound mind with which you can shape your own destiny.

Communicate with anyone you know whom you have unjustly offended and offer sincere apologies. Ask for forgiveness. The more bitter this assignment is, the more you will be free of negative mental influences when you have completed it.

Acknowledge that the space you occupy in this world is in exact ratio to the quantity and quality of the service you render for the benefit of others, plus the mental attitude in which you render it.

Break bad habits. Abstain from your vices one at a time for a month until you show yourself who is boss. If you need help from a counselor or a support group, get it. Don't let your pride master you.

Comprehend that no one can hurt your feelings, make you angry, or frighten you without your full cooperation and consent. Close your mind to anyone who wants to exert a destructive influence.

Perceive that self-pity is an insidious destroyer of self-reliance. Believe that you are the one person on whom you can and should depend at all times.

Relate to every circumstance in your life as something that has happened for the best, for it may be that your saddest experience will bring you your greatest assets if you give time a chance to mellow your distress.

Divert any urge for control over others. Squelch it before it destroys you. Channel that energy into better control over yourself.

Occupy your mind with doing what you want to do so that no time will be left for it to stray to the things you do not want to do.

Attune your mind to attract the things and situations you desire by expressing in a daily prayer your gratitude for what you already have.

Demand a reasonable amount of dividends from life every day, instead of waiting to receive them. You will be surprised to learn how many of the desirable things in life are already yours, even though you have not noticed them.

Live in a style that suits your physical and spiritual requirements, and don't waste time keeping up with the Joneses.

Refuse to heed anyone's advice—unless that person is willing to give you satisfactory evidence of the soundness of his or her counsel. You will save yourself from hucksters, the misguided, and fools.

Discern that personal power does not come from the possession of material things alone. Mahatma Gandhi led his nation to freedom without a fortune.

Exert yourself so that you keep your body in shape. Mental ailments can easily spring from physical ones, and your body, like your mind, must be kept active to remain positive.

Reinforce the habit of tolerance, and keep an open mind on all subjects and toward all people no matter what their race or creed. Learn to like people just as they are, instead of demanding that they be just as you want them to be.

Admit that love is the finest medication for your body and

your soul. Love changes the entire chemistry of your body and conditions it for the expression of a positive mental attitude. It also extends the space you occupy in the hearts of others. The best way to receive love is to give it.

Return every benefit you receive with one of equal or greater value. The Law of Increasing Returns will operate in your favor, and eventually—or perhaps very soon—it will give you the capacity to get everything you are entitled to. A positive mental attitude works both ways.

Avoid the fear of old age by remembering that nothing is ever taken from you without being replaced by something of equal or greater value. Youth, for instance, is replaced by wisdom.

Trust that adequate solutions can be found for all your problems, but accept the fact that the solutions may not always be the ones you want.

Rely on the examples of others to remind you that any disadvantage can be overcome. Thomas Edison had only three months of formal schooling, yet he was the greatest inventor who ever lived; Helen Keller was without sight, hearing, or speech, yet she inspired millions. A definite major purpose is stronger than any limitation.

Welcome friendly criticism instead of reacting to it negatively. Embrace any opportunity to learn how others see you, and use it to take inventory of yourself and look for things which need improvement. Do not fear criticism; encourage it.

Create a mastermind alliance with others dedicated to the principles of success. Discuss your progress and insights and gain the benefit of a much wider range of experience. Always keep these meetings on a positive plane.

Grasp the differences between wishing, hoping, desiring, and having a burning desire to achieve your goal. Only a burning desire gives you a driving motivation, and it can be fueled only by a positive mental attitude.

Abstain from negative conversations, especially carping, gossip, or tearing apart other people's reputations. These activities condition your mind to think negatively.

Discipline your mind to shape your destiny toward whatever purpose in life you have chosen. Seize every one of the benefits in the rewards envelope and make them yours.

Be yourself at all times. Neither you nor anyone else trusts a phony.

Say nothing that does not reflect your positive mental attitude.

Believe in the existence of Infinite Intelligence, which makes it possible for you to draw on all the power you need to take possession of your own mind and direct it toward whatever you choose.

Believe in your ability to become free and self-determining, and put that belief to work by acting upon it. Do it now!

Believe that the American form of government guarantees you the freedom and privileges necessary to pursue your definite major purpose. Work to defend those freedoms as needed.

Believe in the people you are associated with, and recognize that if they are not worthy of your belief, you have the wrong associates.

And finally: read this lesson once a week for six months. You will so thoroughly indoctrinate yourself with these habits and mind conditioners that your mental attitude will become and remain positive at all times.

The 2 Percent Who Succeed

The overwhelming majority of people never recognize the difference between wishing and believing. They never take six steps that will help them use their minds to attain their desires. These steps are summarized below, along with my observations, based on a lifetime of study, of the percentage of people who attain each one.

1. Most people go through life merely *wishing* for things. These wishes are as fleeting as the wind. They have

no power to shape anything. The number of people who stop here: 70 percent.

2. A much smaller percentage develop their wishes into desires. They want the same thing constantly, but that is the end of their commitment. They represent 10 percent.

3. A still smaller percentage develop their wishes and desires into hopes. They dare to imagine, from time to time, that they might get what they seek. I estimate they constitute 8 percent.

4. An even smaller group translates that hope into belief. They expect what they want will actually happen. These people number 6 percent.

5. A smaller group of people crystallize their wishes, desires, and hopes into belief, then into a burning desire, and finally into faith. They constitute 4 percent.

6. Finally, a very few people take the last two steps and then make a plan to get what they want and carry it out. They apply their faith with positive mental attitudes. This group is only 2 percent.

The outstanding leaders in every walk of life are the people in the sixth group. They recognize the power of their own minds; they seize that power and direct it toward whatever they choose. When you take this step, the word "impossible" will have no meaning for you. Everything will be possible for you, and you will manage to get it.

Join the 2 Percent Club

Here are the requirements for membership in the 2 Percent Club. Only you will measure your success in meeting them.

1. Adjust yourself to other people's states of mind and peculiarities so that you can get along peacefully with them. Observe a dog, and learn the art of self-control by

watching how quickly it adjusts itself to its master's moods.

2. Ignore trivial circumstances in your relations with others; do not let them become controversies. Big people look past small slights.

3. Establish control of your mind at the start of each day, using the techniques for building a positive mental attitude. Maintain that attitude throughout the day.

4. Learn the art of selling yourself indirectly, by persuasion and example rather than by the hard sell.

5. Develop a hearty laugh as a means to release anger.

6. Analyze all your setbacks and determine their causes. Discover the seed of equivalent benefit in each circumstance.

7. Concentrate your mind on the can-do portion of the tasks you face. Don't worry about the cannot-do portion unless and until you meet it face-to-face. By that time the can-do portion will have shown you the way to success.

8. Turn all unpleasant circumstances into opportunities for positive action. Make this an automatic habit, and your success will multiply.

9. Remember that no one can win all of the time, no matter how much he deserves it. When you do not get exactly what you wanted, maximize your gain by increasing your understanding of yourself.

10. Look on life as a continuing learning process, and even bad experiences will become good ones.

11. Remember that every thought you release comes back to you multiplied in its effect. Monitor your thoughts, and make sure you send out only those whose fruits you are willing to receive.

12. Avoid associates with negative mental attitudes. Their attitudes will rub off on you and poison every effort you engage in.

13. Be aware of the dual nature of your personality. You have a positive side with a great capacity for belief and a

negative side with an equal capacity for disbelief. Exercise the first, and the second will wither away.

14. Recognize that prayer brings the best results when you have sufficient faith to see yourself already in possession of the things you are praying for. This calls for a positive mental attitude of the highest order.

You can see how a positive mental attitude relies upon and reinforces so many of the principles crucial to personal achievement. You need a definite major purpose, applied faith in that purpose, and the personal initiative to act in ways that express your PMA. The next two chapters will teach you more principles that both support and sustain your PMA. The cultivation of success is a complex, organic process; whenever you advance in acting on one of its tenets, you advance in others.

✦ 8 ✦
CONTROL YOUR ENTHUSIASM

The Benefits of Controlled Enthusiasm
✦
The Dangers of Uncontrolled Enthusiasm
✦
How to Develop Controlled Enthusiasm
✦
Enthusiasm Boosters
✦
Enthusiasm and the Mastermind Alliance
✦
Criticizing Without Destroying Enthusiasm
✦
Enthusiasm Changes Lives

Enthusiasm bears the same relationship to your PMA and your progress toward success as gasoline to a car's engine; it is the fuel that drives things forward.

In working on your PMA, you will learn to control your mind. The same control can be used on your enthusiasm, so that it is continually fed into the cylinders of your mental engine, where it is ignited by the spark of your definite purpose and explodes, pushing the pistons of applied faith and personal initiative.

Enthusiasm is power. With faith, it can transform adversity, failure, and temporary defeat into action. This transmutation depends on your control of your thoughts, for they can just as easily be expressed negatively as positively. By controlling your enthusiasm, you can change any negative expressions and experiences into positive ones. The next chapter on self-discipline will further strengthen your ability to do this.

The Benefits of Controlled Enthusiasm

Controlled enthusiasm has many positive effects. As you develop it, you will:

1. Increase the intensity of your thinking and imagination
2. Acquire a pleasing and convincing tone of voice
3. Reduce the drudgery in your work
4. Have a more attractive personality
5. Gain self-confidence
6. Strengthen your mental and physical health
7. Build your personal initiative
8. Overcome physical and mental fatigue more easily
9. Spread your enthusiasm to others

Enthusiasm stimulates your subconscious mind in much the same way that PMA does. By filling your conscious mind with enthusiasm, you impress upon your subconscious that your burning obsession and your plan for obtaining it are certain things. When your conscious enthusiasm dims, your subconscious will be there, full of images of your success to help you stoke your conscious fires of enthusiasm once again.

The Dangers of Uncontrolled Enthusiasm

Enthusiasm, as I've said, is like gasoline. Properly employed, it can do magnificent things. But if you spill it about carelessly, you run the risk of a catastrophe.

One danger is that your enthusiasm can lead you to monopolize conversation. If you do nothing but talk about yourself, people will tune you out, forget anything worthwhile that you have to say, and refuse to offer you aid and advice when you seek it. How gladly do you suffer bores?

You must also take care that your enthusiasm does not cloud your judgment. Don't reveal your plan to competitors because you think it's so good. If you can see its value, so will others. Don't rush ahead when your plans for your definite purpose call for resources or circumstances that have not appeared.

And don't let your enthusiasm find expression in the wrong things, like roulette wheels or the racetrack. It's fine to enjoy diversions which bring other benefits, like relaxing fishing trips or mind-broadening reading. But if you pour all your enthusiasm into these things, you won't have any left for your definite major purpose, and soon you won't have the resources for your diversions either.

How to Develop Controlled Enthusiasm

Here are the steps to building your enthusiasm:

1. Adopt a definite major purpose.
2. Write out a clear statement of that purpose and your plan for attaining it. Include a statement of what you intend to give in return for its realization.
3. Back your purpose with a burning desire. Fan that desire; coax it; let it become the dominating thought in your mind.
4. Set to work immediately in carrying out your plan.

5. Follow your plan accurately and persistently.

6. If you are overtaken by defeat, study your plan carefully, and change it if necessary. Do not change it simply because you have met defeat.

7. Ally yourself with others whose aid you need.

8. Keep away from joy-killers and naysayers. Stick with the optimists.

9. *Never let a day pass without devoting some time to furthering your plan.* You are developing enthusiasm as a habit, and habits require reinforcement.

10. Keep yourself sold on the idea that you will obtain your definite major purpose, no matter how far away that moment seems. Autosuggestion is a powerful force in developing enthusiasm.

11. Keep your mind positive at all times. Enthusiasm will not thrive in a field full of fear, envy, greed, jealousy, doubt, revenge, hatred, intolerance, and procrastination. It needs positive thought and action.

Does this list sound like things you are already doing? It should. Enthusiasm is the natural outgrowth of all your efforts toward success. What is important is that you now recognize that every appropriate move you make is building your enthusiasm as well. Examine each move for the presence of enthusiasm. Understand how it has helped you, and you will be in a better position to apply this tool consciously when you need it.

Enthusiasm Boosters

If you think that your enthusiasm needs work, that it hasn't been growing apace with your progress on the other principles, you can stimulate it with some simple exercises.

To Be Enthusiastic, Act Enthusiastically

Does this advice seem redundant? It isn't. If you enter a meeting with your enthusiasm low, ignore it. Shake hands confidently; reply definitively to questions; assert the value of your ideas and proposals. Ideally, enthusiasm makes these things automatic, but if you consciously perform the actions, you will begin to see their positive results. This stokes the fires of enthusiasm.

Keep an Enthusiasm Log

When your enthusiasm runs high, make a note of it in a notebook. Write down the circumstances that inspired you and the manifestations of that enthusiasm. Were you spurred to action? Did you solve a problem? Did you persuade someone of something? Also, keep a written copy of your definite major purpose and your plan for it inside your notebook. Then, whenever your enthusiasm is ebbing, pick up your valuable book. Not only will it remind you of the reason you should be enthusiastic, but it will also review for you the benefits of that enthusiasm. Enthusiasm is a spiral, turning inward or outward, rising or falling. To give your enthusiasm a push in the right direction, refer to your notebook when the spiral is collapsing in on itself.

Complete a Can-do Task

In a way, can-do tasks are like crutches, but when you aren't moving the way you should be, you're not helping yourself by not using them. These are things that you know you can complete quickly and well. They should be somehow related to your definite major purpose, so that they help direct and control your enthusiasm.

For instance, suppose that you own a hardware store. Your responsibilities may not have you on the floor very often; instead you're in the back office. But you remember how much you enjoyed working on the sales floor. Go back to that floor; make a few sales; renew your enthusiasm by returning to its roots.

A word of warning: If you have to resort to enthusiasm boosters frequently, something is wrong. You have strayed from the definite purpose you were pursuing. You will need to take a serious look at your plan for that purpose and think about realigning it so that it reflects your ambitions more closely.

Enthusiasm and the Mastermind Alliance

One of the most important places where your enthusiasm will go to work is in your mastermind alliance. If you share your enthusiasm with the other members, you will increase theirs. They, in turn, will be able to feed and support your enthusiasm.

Sometimes all members of the group benefit equally from this process. But it is more likely that you, as the leader, will benefit most. The Law of Increasing Returns will reward you for your initial, originating enthusiasm in a way that far exceeds either your own contributions or the dividends paid to the other members.

Increased enthusiasm in your alliance will mean increased faith as well. With that additional faith will come more insight into Infinite Intelligence and thus more creativity. Other ways to increase your own and your alliance's creativity are discussed in Chapter 14.

Criticizing Without Destroying Enthusiasm

Sometimes it will be necessary to criticize members of your mastermind alliance or the people working for you who are not carrying their share of the load. You can do this without destroying their enthusiasm if you use a careful process. You must lead your "black sheep" to admit their mistakes on their own.

Here's an example of that process, taught me by Andrew Carnegie:

My personal secretary was a young man who had been with me for several years. He was efficient, dependable and had a pleasing personality. He became associated with a group of people who had the bad habit of getting their enthusiasm out of a whiskey bottle. The first thing I knew he began to show up late on Monday mornings. Then he became irritable, and I knew the time had come for me to do a little friendly analysis on his behalf. So I prepared the way by inviting him to my home for dinner.

During the meal we chatted pleasantly about everything except the subject I had in mind discussing with him. After dinner we went to the library and lighted our cigars. The stage was then set, so I began by asking him a few questions.

First I asked him if he believed a man who was a regular drinker should be considered for a promotion, and he replied that he thought not.

Then I asked him what he would do if he had in his employ a man so addicted to drink that he could not get to work on time, and he replied that he would probably fire him.

By this time he had begun to squirm in his chair, and I waited a while to give him the chance to do some serious thinking. Then I asked him if he thought it might be possible for a sensible man to change his habits in time to save himself from ruin.

He waited for a couple of minutes before answering, then straightened up, looked me squarely in the eyes and said:

"You needn't go any further. I have known for a long time that this hour was coming, and I deeply appreciate your kindness in making it as easy as possible. All I can say is that I have been a fool, but I can change, and I will do so if you bear with me long enough to let me prove it."

So he was disciplined, but it was with self-discipline. He took hold of his job with renewed enthusiasm and promoted himself from one position to another until he became manager of one of our largest steel plants.

You can see the value and importance of this kind of approach. If Carnegie had angrily confronted this man, no doubt the fellow would have been so ashamed he would have denied any problem. Carnegie would have lost a valuable employee, and the man would have been driven only deeper into his destructive habits. Instead both men came out ahead.

Respect and nurture the enthusiasm others have. It can overcome powerful problems, and from those problems it will extract benefits beyond your imagination.

Enthusiasm Changes Lives

Another person's enthusiasm was what set me moving toward the success I have attained. That person was my stepmother.

I was nine years old when she entered our home. We lived in poverty in rural Virginia, but she had come from better circumstances, and she would not accept our circumstances without protest.

My father introduced me to her with these words: "I would like you to meet the fellow who is distinguished for being the worst boy in this county and will probably start throwing rocks at you no later than tomorrow morning."

My stepmother walked over to me, tilted my head upward, and looked me right in the eye. Then she looked at my father and replied, "You are wrong. This is not the worst boy in the county, but the smartest one who hasn't yet found an outlet for his enthusiasm."

That statement began a friendship between us which was destined to produce these Seventeen Principles of Success and to carry their influence around the world. No one had ever called me smart. My family and neighbors had built me up in my own mind as being a bad boy, and I had done nothing to disappoint them. My stepmother, in one brief statement, changed all that.

She changed many things. She persuaded my father to go to dental school, from which he was graduated with honors. She moved our family into the county seat, where my father's practice could flourish and my brothers and I could be better educated. My father resisted these efforts at first, but her enthusiasm always won him over.

When I turned fourteen, she bought me a secondhand typewriter and told me that she believed that I could become a writer. I knew her enthusiasm, I relished it, and I saw how it had already improved our lives. I accepted her belief and began to write for local newspapers. I was doing the same kind of writing that fateful day I went to interview Andrew Carnegie and received the charge that became my life's work. My stepmother's enthusiasm had not just put me in a position to grasp such an opportunity but given me the self-confidence and enthusiasm of my own to succeed at it.

I wasn't the only benefactor. My father became the most prosperous man in town. My brothers and stepbrothers became a physician, a dentist, a lawyer, and a college president.

What power enthusiasm has! When that power is released to support definiteness of purpose and is constantly renewed by faith, it becomes an irresistible force for which poverty and temporary defeat are no match.

You can communicate that power to anyone who needs it. This is probably the greatest work you can do with your enthusiasm. Excite the imaginations of others; inspire their creative vision; help them connect with Infinite Intelligence.

Building, demonstrating, and sharing enthusiasm are a perfect manifestation of the moral principles behind the science of success. When you deliver your work with enthusiasm, you are already going the extra mile. You create a success consciousness around you that inevitably affects others for the better. The more enthusiasm you direct into the world, the better you are preparing yourself to attain exactly what you want.

◆ 9 ◆
ENFORCE
SELF-DISCIPLINE

Controlling Your Emotions
◆
The Big Four
◆
The Power of Self-Discipline
◆
The Structure of Your Mind
◆
The Things You Cannot Discipline
◆
The Power of the Will

Earlier chapters have placed heavy emphasis on the importance of taking control of your mind. This control is pivotal to your personal initiative, positive mental attitude, and controlled enthusiasm. Self-discipline is the process that ties all these efforts together for you.

It isn't possible to achieve self-discipline without making some progress on those other principles; self-discipline requires self-knowledge and an accurate assessment of your current abilities. Likewise, the other principles can't really be put into action without self-discipline. It is the channel through which all your personal power for success must flow.

Think of your mind as a reservoir in which you have been storing up potential power. You will now learn to release that power in precise quantities and specific directions. This is the essence of self-discipline.

Controlling Your Emotions

Most people act first and think about the consequences later. Self-discipline will reverse that process. You will learn to think before you act.

The primary means to this end is your control of your emotions. For review, the fourteen major emotions are repeated below.

Positive Emotions	Negative Emotions
1. Love	1. Fear
2. Sex	2. Jealousy
3. Hope	3. Hatred
4. Faith	4. Revenge
5. Enthusiasm	5. Greed
6. Loyalty	6. Anger
7. Desire	7. Superstition

All these emotions are states of mind and are thus subject to your control. You can see right away how dangerous the negative emotions can be if they are not mastered. The positive emotions can also be destructive if you do not organize and release them with conscious control.

Inherent in these emotions is explosive power. If you regulate that power properly, it can lift you to the heights of achievement. But if you let it run wild, it can dash you to pieces on the rocks of failure.

You learned in earlier chapters that a definite major purpose, activated by a driving motive, is the starting point of all worthwhile achievement. This motive must be so strong that it will subordinate all your thoughts and efforts to the attainment of your definite purpose. But your drive—your emotions—must also be subject to your own good judgment so that your enthusiasm and desire will not run over your wisdom. In other words, you must discipline yourself so that your drive is always under control and directed in the proper channels.

Self-discipline calls for balancing your emotions with your reasoning. This means you must learn to consult both your feelings and your reason before you reach any decision. Sometimes you will need to set aside your emotions and follow the dictates of reason alone. Other times you will decide in favor of your emotions, modified by your reason. A happy medium is important.

Consider, for example, those people who are so in love that they will do anything for their beloveds. They are putty in the hands of others. They rarely amount to anything because they have no purposes of their own in life.

You might wonder if this danger means that it would be safer and wiser to control your life strictly on the basis of reason and leave emotion out of every decision. The answer is an emphatic no.

Don't forget, your emotions provide your driving power, the activating force which enables you to put your decisions into action. If you destroyed hope and faith, what would there be to live for? If you killed enthusiasm, loyalty, and desire but still retained reason, what good would reason be? It would still be there to provide direction, but what would it direct?

You must control and direct your emotions, not abolish them. Besides, abolition would be an impossible task. Emotions are like a river. Their power can be dammed up and released under control and direction, but it cannot be held forever in check. Sooner or later the dam will burst, unleashing catastrophic destruction.

Your negative emotions can also be controlled and directed. PMA and self-discipline can remove their harmful effects and make them serve constructive purposes. Sometimes fear and anger will inspire intense action. But you must always submit your negative emotions—and your positive ones—to the examination of your reason before releasing them. Emotion without reason is a dreadful enemy.

What faculty provides the crucial balance between emotion and reason? It is your willpower, or ego, a subject which will be explored in more detail below. Self-discipline will teach you to throw your willpower behind either reason or emotion and amplify the intensity of their expression.

Both your heart and your mind need a master, and they can find that master in your ego. However, your ego will fill this role only if you use self-discipline. In the absence of self-discipline, your mind and heart will fight their battles as they please. In this situation the person within whose mind the fight is carried out often gets badly hurt.

The Big Four

Your self-discipline will not only control your emotions and balance your reason but also be incredibly useful in four highly important areas.

Appetite

Too much food, drink, and other outside influences—such as drugs—which are bad for your body can shorten your life, sap your energy, and distract you from the work at hand. It isn't necessary to moralize on these points. The empirical effects of not being in control of your appetite are sufficient cause for you to subject your appetites to self-discipline.

Positive Mental Attitude

PMA is the only frame of mind in which you can have definiteness of purpose. Through it you can induce others to cooperate with you and help you; it can also attract the power of Infinite Intelligence by applying your faith. Self-discipline ensures that you use your mental attitude to attract the things you want and to repel the things that threaten you.

Time

There is an old saying: "Wasting time is sinful." Most people waste enough time in gossip alone to earn them all the luxuries they envy in others. Time is your most precious asset. If used correctly, it is like money in the bank. You must spend it under strict self-discipline. One of the easiest ways to do this is to schedule your time use for the next twenty-four hours, and stick to that chart. Do it once, and it will be easier the next time.

Aleksandr Solzhenitsyn is another example of someone whose self-discipline allowed him to have an enormous impact. Not only did he survive years in Soviet gulags and then dare to write about it, he kept to a rigorous schedule of writing even after being exiled to the United States. Though he was an international celebrity and could have spent the rest of his life basking in attention, Solzhenitsyn moved to a small town in Vermont so he could find solitude.

Until he returned to Russia to participate in the reform of the country, he would get up at six and begin to write after eating a small breakfast. He would stop for a short lunch, then begin writing again, often until late in the evening and sometimes until the sun rose again. He didn't allow the telephone to interrupt his work and he rarely even left home. The result was a series of novels called *The Red Wheel*, a historical epic of tremendous importance.

Even when history finally caught up with his Soviet oppressors, Solzhenitsyn resisted the urge to rush back to Moscow because he knew he had to finish his work. He didn't let countless opportunities to appear on news programs—which would have gained publicity for his books and made him money—distract him from the job at hand. His self-discipline, honed during his years in the gulags, allowed him

to finish what he had started and made him a powerful figure when the Soviet empire finally collapsed.

Definiteness of Purpose

The importance of definiteness of purpose had better be
clear to you by now. You know that it is the beginning of all
achievements when it is tied to a strong, compelling motive.
If you haven't yet made up your mind about your definite
purpose, go back to the first chapter, and write out your major objective in life and your plans for attaining it. This is the
first step in self-discipline. Even Infinite Intelligence can't
help you get where you're going if you haven't made up
your mind about exactly where you want to go.

There's an old joke about a preacher who was stranded on
the roof of his church in a flood. As the waters rose higher
around him, he prayed fervently for God to rescue him. "The
Lord will provide," he told himself.

Soon a boat floated by. The occupants called to the preacher
to swim to them. "Don't worry about me," the preacher called
back. "The Lord will provide." Reluctantly the people on the
boat went on.

The waters rose higher and soon were lapping around the
knees of the man of God. Another boat appeared within a
few yards of the church rooftop. The rescuers inside called to
the preacher, and again he replied, "The Lord will provide!"
This boat went on, and the preacher prayed even more fervently.

Just as the water reached the preacher's chin, a third boat
appeared. It came so close that the preacher could have
jumped right in. But the terrified man clutched his steeple
and cried, "Save someone else. The Lord will provide for
me!" And the boat went on.

Within a few minutes the waters closed over the preacher's head, and he drowned. Reaching the gates of heaven, he
asked for an immediate audience with the Lord, which was

granted. In the divine presence the preacher humbled himself and asked, "Heavenly Father, my work on earth was not yet finished. Why didn't you save me?"

"Good grief" came the reply. "I thought you *wanted* to come here. I sent you three boats, didn't I?"

Self-discipline makes you jump when your boat comes by.

The Power of Self-Discipline

When you speak of power, you usually think of a Rockefeller or a Trump, somebody with money or property. But one of the most powerful men who ever lived had neither. Mahatma Gandhi didn't own a house, he had no money, but his influence eclipses that of any other person of this century.

That's an astounding statement until you look at it and analyze the source of Gandhi's power. Here was a man who over long years, step by step, defeated the British Empire. He wrested freedom for India from the British by using a power His Majesty's Government didn't understand. There were five sources to his power:

Definiteness of purpose. Gandhi's purpose was to free the people of India. He knew precisely what he wanted, what his major aim in life was, and he was determined that nothing would defeat him.

Going the extra mile. No one asked Gandhi to spend his life as he did; no one paid him to do so. He did not have a selfish purpose; he did not think in terms of personal reward. He went not only the extra mile but many millions of extra miles because he was planning to benefit the four hundred million people living in his country. No wonder he had power.

Applied faith. Gandhi completely cleared his mind of any doubt that he would eventually win the freedom he desired for his people. He kept his mind securely fixed on his definite major purpose. And this resolute purpose and his persistent action to achieve it opened his mind to the power of Infinite Intelligence.

Mastermind. Gandhi assembled what is probably the greatest mastermind alliance in human history. It consisted of hundreds of millions of minds. Many of these minds may have been lacking in formal education, but each had the capacity for faith and a burning desire to achieve the goal of freedom Gandhi was leading it toward. No power in the world could have defeated such a powerful mastermind alliance—except an even larger one.

Self-discipline. How do you suppose Gandhi managed to keep his mind focused on one definite major purpose all those years? He must have had many opportunities to capitalize on his situation or to use his power for his personal benefit. Anyone who had the power Gandhi had might have been tempted by such opportunities. But he had the self-discipline to lead a simple life, and thus he had the self-discipline to free a nation.

The Structure of Your Mind

Your mind is divided into six departments which are subject to your conscious control. Understanding these departments helps you understand self-discipline.

On pages 116 and 117 you will find two charts which diagram the thinking process. Chart One shows the six departments which you can control. Chart Two shows the mechanism by which they operate.

The six departments are:

1. The ego. The source of willpower. It acts as a supreme court, with the power to reverse, modify, change, or eliminate the entire work of all the other departments.

2. Emotions. Here is generated the driving force which sets your thoughts, plans, and purposes into action.

3. Reason. This is where you weigh, eliminate, and

properly evaluate the products of your imagination and emotions.

4. Imagination. This is where you create ideas, plans, and methods of attaining your desired ends.

5. Conscience. Here you test the moral justice of your thoughts, plans, and purposes.

6. The memory. This acts as the keeper of records of all your experiences and as a storehouse for all sense perceptions and inspiration from Infinite Intelligence.

The Ego

The ego, seat of your willpower, is the most valuable thing your body possesses. The rest of you is a collection of chemicals which, on the open market, aren't worth the price of dinner in a decent restaurant. You must control and discipline this priceless part of yourself. It can stand for anything you value, from poverty and ill health to your brightest ambitions.

Some egos are weak and lacking in courage. Some are overinflated. Neither kind amounts to anything, but most people struggle with weak ones.

Don't let a weak ego hold you back. A prosperous man I knew suffered a defeat in business and ended up driving a taxicab for a few hundred dollars a week. There's nothing wrong with driving a taxicab, but it isn't the right kind of employment for someone who was making six figures. That man needed to bolster his ego so he could return to success.

One woman I know wore a huge diamond ring on her finger. That ring was a symbol of her success, not a sign of vanity or ostentation. Once she had been poor, but with that ring on her finger she constantly reminded her ego that her poverty was of the past. She fed her ego with images that strengthened it. That is just what you must do with your ego. It may not require something as visible—and expensive—as a diamond ring, but it requires sustenance.

Always treat your ego as your most precious possession,

CHART NO. 1

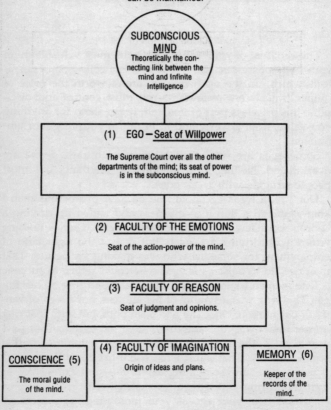

THE SIX DEPARTMENTS of THE MIND over which Self-discipline
can be maintained.

**SUBCONSCIOUS
MIND**
Theoretically the con-
necting link between the
mind and Infinite
Intelligence

(1) EGO — Seat of Willpower

The Supreme Court over all the other
departments of the mind; its seat of power
is in the subconscious mind.

(2) FACULTY OF THE EMOTIONS

Seat of the action-power of the mind.

(3) FACULTY OF REASON

Seat of judgment and opinions.

CONSCIENCE (5)

The moral guide
of the mind.

(4) FACULTY OF IMAGINATION

Origin of ideas and plans.

MEMORY (6)

Keeper of the
records of the
mind.

CHART NO. 2

Ten factors that constitute the mechanism of thought. Note that the subconscious section of the mind has access to all departments of the mind, <u>but is not under the control of any.</u>

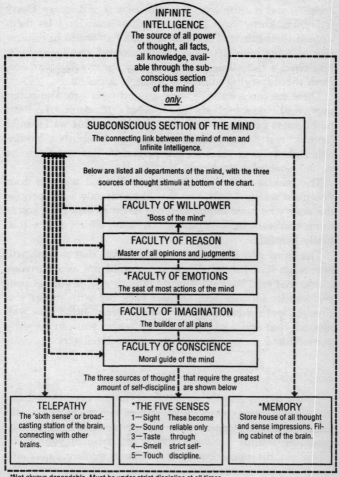

INFINITE INTELLIGENCE
The source of all power of thought, all facts, all knowledge, available through the subconscious section of the mind *only*.

SUBCONSCIOUS SECTION OF THE MIND
The connecting link between the mind of men and Infinite Intelligence.

Below are listed all departments of the mind, with the three sources of thought stimuli at bottom of the chart.

FACULTY OF WILLPOWER
"Boss of the mind"

FACULTY OF REASON
Master of all opinions and judgments

***FACULTY OF EMOTIONS**
The seat of most actions of the mind

FACULTY OF IMAGINATION
The builder of all plans

FACULTY OF CONSCIENCE
Moral guide of the mind

The three sources of thought that require the greatest amount of self-discipline are shown below

TELEPATHY
The "sixth sense" or broadcasting station of the brain, connecting with other brains.

***THE FIVE SENSES**
1— Sight   These become
2— Sound   reliable only
3— Taste   through
4— Smell   strict self-
5— Touch   discipline.

***MEMORY**
Store house of all thought and sense impressions. Filing cabinet of the brain.

*Not always dependable. Must be under strict discipline at all times.

and protect it as if it were a diamond. You certainly wouldn't leave a diamond around for anyone to pick up. Yet most people leave their egos wide open for anyone to come in and pollute with thoughts of fear and worry. Don't let others know your secret thoughts, and don't let them unload their burdens on you. You can't afford to have worries of your own, let alone carry around someone else's. You need a technique to protect your inner self, your ego, from the damaging effects of negative ideas.

There are three walls to build around your ego. The outermost wall is just high enough to keep out people who have no business getting in to take up your time. This wall should have several doors, and if someone can establish a reasonable right to your time, let that person in. But make sure he or she establishes that right first.

The middle wall is much taller, and it has a single door you must watch closely. You should admit only a few people, the ones who have established the fact that they have something you want or something in common which will be mutually helpful.

The third and innermost wall is so tall that no one will ever scale it; it has no doors. You should not allow anyone inside that wall because it protects your ego. If you let people wander in, they will wander back out with things you cherish, leaving behind worry and anxiety. Build this wall around your ego, and make a place where you can retire by yourself and communicate with Infinite Intelligence.

Emotions

Earlier in this chapter we talked about the need for balancing your emotions with the faculty of reason. Here we will look at a different aspect of the emotions. Consider for a moment the serious problems which can arise in your mind when old disappointments and failures surface again and again in your emotions.

Self-discipline is the only real solution to such problems. It begins with the recognition that there are only two kinds of problems: those you can solve and those you can't.

Problems that can be solved should immediately be dealt with by the most practical means available. This is why you were told in an earlier chapter to make amends for old wrongs you may have done. Problems which can't be solved should be put out of your mind and forgotten.

Think of this forgetting as closing the door on whatever it is that disturbs your emotional equilibrium. Self-discipline allows you to close this door and lock it securely, instead of standing in the door and looking wistfully back at what might have been. Look forward instead into the future.

One method is to visualize some symbol of the unsolvable problem floating deep in space. Imagine a giant envelope opening next to that symbol and the symbol sliding gently into that envelope. Let the envelope close, and then watch it drift away into the void.

Whether you close a door or dispatch an envelope, you are employing a valuable technique. It requires a good, strong will, and repeated practice of this process only strengthens your will.

Door closing does not make you hard, cold, or unemotional, but it does require firmness. Self-discipline cannot permit lurking memories, and you cannot waste time worrying over the unsolvable. Doing so destroys your creative force, undermines your initiative, disturbs your faculty of reason, and just plain confuses all the departments of your mind.

Closing the door on fear and worry allows you to open the doors of hope and faith.

Reason

If your ego functions as a supreme court, your reason functions as a superior court, handling the more routine functions of judgment. It evaluates the creations of the imag-

ination, modifies the expression of the emotions, and ratifies
the decisions of the conscience. You train your rational faculties by observation, study, and analysis of truth.

Imagination

Your imagination is responsible for all creative effort. New
ideas are assembled here, and you must allow your reason to
control its activities carefully. Keep your imagination workshop focused on things related to your definite major purpose, not on fantasies about winning the lottery. Because
imagination is responsible for creating everything new in the
world, it is an invaluable tool for your progress along the
path to success.

Conscience

Your conscience keeps an eye on the moral justice of all
your thoughts and deeds. If you always consult it and heed
its advice, it will repay you by keeping you honorable and
esteemed by others. If you ignore its advice, be careful. At
the least you will alienate the members of your mastermind
alliance, cut yourself off from the power of Infinite Intelligence, and be plagued by countless fears. At the worst you
will discover that society has built many special rooms for
people who don't obey their consciences. The view from
these rooms is usually obstructed by bars.

The Memory

Here you store all the impressions of both your conscious
and subconscious minds. Self-discipline will allow you to
keep unpleasant memories tucked away, after you have
learned the lessons those memories inspire. Many positive
things may also be stored in your memory, ready to be called
forth upon demand by a willpower strengthened by self-
discipline.

Your self-discipline is the procedure you use to coordinate these departments of your mind and keep each of them under control. Its most immediate effect is the mental harmony you need to focus all your efforts toward success.

The Things You Cannot Discipline

There are four other elements that play a role in your mental process but that you cannot control. You must learn to understand them and adapt to their ways.

Infinite Intelligence

The chapter on applied faith explains the power and importance of Infinite Intelligence. You cannot discipline it; instead you must discipline yourself to be ready to receive it and to act on its wisdom.

The Subconscious

You cannot directly control your subconscious; that's a big part of what its name implies. It acts only in response to stimulus from your emotions, but these *are* something you can control through self-discipline. When your emotions are positive and directed toward a definite purpose, your subconscious will be powerfully and similarly affected. However, it will respond just as quickly to negative emotions; it can't distinguish between the two. This is why your self-discipline must be applied to your emotions, so that your subconscious works for you, not against you.

Telepathy

Telepathy is the broadcasting of your mental attitudes and thoughts to others. I'm not talking about such mundane uses as telling the baby-sitter when to put the kids to bed while you're out at the movies. I'm referring to the mental communication that develops between you and others committed to similar purposes. Your mastermind alliance is the best example of this power. As your alliance grows, each member will learn to anticipate the ideas of others and to connect immediately with their intense enthusiasm and inspiration. You can't control this process, but your self-discipline will aid you in cultivating the positive qualities which bring it into play.

The Senses

Sight, sound, taste, smell, and touch all may deceive you. They are capable only of perceiving the obvious. Much of what goes on in this world is not obvious, and the senses are easily fooled. While you can, to an extent, train your senses to serve you better, you must always evaluate the messages you receive from them by applying your reason.

All four of these things must be a part of your mental processes. Your self-discipline will not give you direct authority over them, but it can—and must—make you more aware of their operations at all times.

The Power of the Will

The greatest manifestation of self-discipline is in the strength of your will. As I have pointed out, your will is the supreme court of your mind. It may have the theoretical authority to order all your mental processes, but that authority depends upon constant, consistent, and ethical exercise.

The power of a will trained by self-discipline is an irresistible force. The only limit on that power is the one that you impose on it by restricting or ignoring your self-discipline.

History and folklore are full of stories of people whose wills alone triumphed over death and other incredible adversities. Who remembers the people whose weak wills kept them mired in mediocrity?

✦ 10 ✦

THINK ACCURATELY

The Raw Power of Thought
✦
The Focused Power of Accurate Thought
✦
The Thinking Process
✦
Techniques for Evaluation
✦
The Sources of Your Thought Habits
✦
Two Big Mistakes
✦
Controlled Habits

Think of your mind as a piece of land. Through diligent, planned work, it can be cultivated into a beautiful and productive garden. Or it can lie fallow, overrun by weeds sprouting from seed carried by passing birds and the wind.

Harvesting the bounty of your mind depends on careful effort and preparation by you, the gardener. This organization and its successful implementation are the result of accurate thinking.

All plans, purposes, and achievements are created by thought. Your thoughts, you have already learned, are the only thing over which you have complete control. You can use them wisely or unwisely, but however you do it, your thoughts have power.

The Raw Power of Thought

An unknown paperhanger used thought powerfully. He sat moodily in a prison cell, contemplating the fact that life offered some people power and riches, while he was confined for a time. His very act of thought changed his life.

The next the world heard of this man, he had written a book in which he frankly revealed the purposes of his mind and put the world on notice of his specific goal in life. Some people read the book and smiled tolerantly; others didn't even bother since they thought it was the work of a lunatic.

A little more than a decade later this madman had half of Europe under his heel and the other half frightened out of its wits and fighting for dear life. His actions were setting the world on fire, but people in America went complacently about their business, believing that the fire would burn itself out.

Adolf Hitler found the opportunity to use his power so destructively because so many other people failed to use theirs constructively. Although his thinking was not accurate in the sense that you will come to understand, it still had the power to cause death and suffering for countless millions of innocent people. His thoughts were abominations, but they had force.

Applied accurate thinking is crucial to your desire for success, but you should also recognize that exercising it is a moral duty you owe to every other person in the world.

The Focused Power of Accurate Thought

Every story you have read in this book about a successful person proves the benefits—individual and social—of accurate thought harnessed to a worthy definite purpose.

The rigor of Jonas Salk's thinking discovered the vaccine which prevents polio. George C. Marshall's careful planning revitalized Europe economically after the effects of Hitler's inhuman atrocities. George Bush's methodical assembly of the Desert Storm alliance and the detailed planning of generals like Norman Schwarzkopf and Colin Powell put a stop to Saddam Hussein's Hitler-like ambitions. The quiet diligence that Mother Clara Hale put into building Harlem's Hale House now provides love and care to children ravaged by their parents' addiction to drugs and infection with AIDS.

None of these great things could ever have happened without accurate thinking. You can never achieve anything great without learning to think accurately.

The Thinking Process

Accurate thinking is based on two types of reasoning:

1. Induction. This is the act of reasoning from a part to a whole, from the particular to the general, from the individual to the universal. It is based on experience and experimentation and draws conclusions from them.

2. Deduction. In this act of reasoning specific conclusions are based on general logical assumptions.

The two types of reasoning are very different, but they can work together.

For instance, suppose that every time you throw a rock at a window, the window breaks while the rock remains unchanged. The results of your repeated efforts cause you to reason inductively that the glass is fragile and that the rock is not.

From this inductive reasoning, you can then proceed to deductive reasoning, which would suggest to you, among other things, that another nonfragile object—a baseball, for example—would also break the glass or that the rock might also penetrate other fragile things like paper.

Of course, your reasoning in this case would be limited since you have not accounted for many variables. A fragile object could also break the window (certainly a bottle could), and some fragile objects like cloth might simply collapse about a thrown rock instead of breaking. I'm sure you can think of many other contingencies which would apply in this case.

This example shows how easy it is to make false conclusions and why accurate thinking is important and why your reasoning must be rigorous. You must examine the results of your reasoning consistently and look for flaws. You should apply this process just as stringently to the thinking of other people.

To be an accurate thinker, you must take two important steps:

1. Separate facts from opinions, fictions, unproved hypotheses, and hearsay.
2. Separate facts into two categories: important and unimportant.

Everyone except accurate thinkers has an overabundance of opinions, and these are usually worthless. Many of them can be dangerous and destructive, especially when they occur in conjunction with personal initiative. Hitler is an obvious example.

You cannot accept an opinion offered to you unless it is based on facts or sound hypotheses about the facts. You should not offer any opinions except on the same grounds. Accurate thinkers never act on freely offered opinions without giving them the closest scrutiny; they permit no one to do their thinking for them. They obtain facts, information, and counsel from others, but they retain the right to accept or reject it in whole or in part.

Newspapers, gossip, and rumor are unreliable sources from which to procure facts, as the events they cover are so changeable and these particular media are often not subject to verification. Remember the famous headline DEWEY DEFEATS TRUMAN? If you had believed it, you would probably still be wondering why General MacArthur lost his job.

Wishes are often fathers to popularly accepted "facts" since people naturally assume facts to be things that harmonize with their wishes. But these kinds of "facts" are so freely offered that you should remember that real facts generally have a price tag attached—the price of the painstaking labor needed to examine them for accuracy.

For a few days not so long ago our nation was in the grip of the rumor that hypodermic needles were appearing in Pepsi cans everywhere. There were reports of incidents from more than twenty states. On the basis of this "fact," the price of Pepsi stock dropped dramatically, and many investors sold Pepsico shares for much less than they had paid for them, even though the company's executives assured the country that this kind of tampering was highly unlikely.

Accurate thinkers recognized the improbability of such a widespread tampering scheme and bought Pepsi stock. Then the FDA and the FBI declared every single report to be a hoax.

Who benefited? The panicky sellers who had bought "high" and then prematurely sold a very solid company or the accurate thinkers who bought the stock at a discount price?

Techniques for Evaluation

As an accurate thinker you must scrutinize every bit of information you encounter. You have to realize that some things contain facts while being colored, modified, or exaggerated, either intentionally or carelessly. Any political campaign will demonstrate this point in glorious detail.

You should apply some tests to information you encounter. If you read a book, for example, you should ask questions like these:

1. Is the writer a recognized authority on the subject covered?

2. Did the writer have a motive in writing the book other than imparting accurate information? What is that motive?

3. Does the writer have a profit interest in the subject covered?

4. Is the writer a person of sound judgment or a fanatic?

5. Are there easily accessible sources to check and verify the writer's statements?

6. Do the writer's statements harmonize with common sense and experience?

Before you accept anyone's statements as facts, you must try to find the motive behind those statements. The motive can be completely honorable, but you must still be careful about accepting the statements of overzealous people who have a habit of letting their emotions run wild. Honor alone does not equal accuracy.

You must rely upon your own judgment and be cautious no matter who is trying to influence you. If a statement does not seem reasonable or contradicts your experience, set it aside for further examination.

When you ask others for facts or judgments, try not to disclose the answer you expect or your motives in asking, for people often alter their advice to fit what they assume is their listener's desire. This process may be innocent or duplicitous, but you should avoid it. Instead of asking, "Do you think it would be possible to send a man to Saturn?" or "How can I send a man to Saturn?" ask, "What do you know about the possibility of sending a man to Saturn?" or even better, "What do you know about space travel?" This example may seem a little absurd, but if you substitute "moon" for "Saturn" in the above sentences, you'll see evidence of the power of accurate thinking.

The Sources of Your Thought Habits

Your initial thought habits come from two sources, both of them hereditary:

1. Physical heredity. The nature and character of the generations that preceded you have some influence on your thought habits. You may be born with a predominantly rigid or free-floating thinking process, which many scientists now categorize as left- or right-brained. The first emphasizes details; the other, broad schemes. Accurate thinking can modify, strengthen, and direct both qualities, since everyone possesses each, even though one is stronger than the other.

2. Social heredity. Your environmental influences, education, and experience all are social stimuli. Thinking is most influenced by these things, and that is dangerous because it means that much of your thinking is inspired by others. However, you can take action to control and select these influences, such as reading this book.

Most people embrace a religion, ally themselves politically, even select the car they drive not because they have given thought to the subject but because of the influences of those nearest them: friends, relatives, and acquaintances.

As an accurate thinker you will accept no political, religious, or other type of thought, regardless of its source, unless and until you have carefully analyzed it. Then you will accept it or reject it of your own free will, and its value to you will be much greater.

Robert Taylor, onetime governor of Tennessee, once asked a young man why he was a confirmed Democrat. "Because," the young man exclaimed, "I live in Tennessee, and my father and grandfather are Democrats. That's why!"

"Well," said the governor, "wouldn't you be in a bad fix if your father and grandfather had been horse thieves?"

I don't care what your party is, but you must select it, as you select everything, on the basis of accurate thought, not on the habits of others.

Two Big Mistakes

Two opposite qualities are very prevalent in human nature, but each is a major roadblock to accurate thinking.

Credulousness—the habit of believing on the basis of little or no evidence—is a major human fault, for it is fatal to accuracy in thinking. This fault—in both his own people and those of the world—certainly let Hitler build his influence to such horrendous levels. The mind of an accurate thinker is an eternal question mark. You must challenge everyone and everything that influences it.

This does not imply a lack of faith. In fact, it is the greatest expression of respect for the Creator since you recognize that your thoughts are the only thing over which you have been given complete control and you embrace this blessing.

The small minority of accurate thinkers has always been the hope of humanity. For they are the pioneers in whatever they do. They create business and industry, advance science and education, and inspire invention and religion. Emerson said it best:

Beware when the great God lets loose a thinker on this planet. Then all things are at risk. It is as when a conflagration has broken out in a great city, and no man knows what is safe or where it will end. There is not a piece of science but its flank may be turned tomorrow; there is not literary reputation, not the so-called eternal names of fame, that may not be revised and condemned. The very hopes of man, the thoughts of his heart, the religion of nations, the manners and morals of mankind, are all at the mercy of a new generalization. Generalization is always a new influx of the Divinity into the mind. Hence the thrill that attends it.

When you are an accurate thinker, you are the master, not the slave, of your emotions. You live among other people without giving them the power to control your thinking. You must always be on guard against the human tendency initially to reject an idea because it is unsound but, by close association with it in the form of family, friends, and coworkers, to endure it, then to embrace it as your own, forgetting its original source and your first evaluation of it.

Your mind will absorb any idea that it is repeatedly subjected to, whether good or bad, right or wrong. As an accurate thinker you can make this trait work for you in the sense that whatever you think today becomes what you are tomorrow. This is the essence of the power of a definite major purpose and positive mental attitude.

The other common weakness in most people's thinking is a tendency to disbelieve anything they do not understand.

When the Wright brothers announced that they had built a machine that could fly and asked newspaper reporters to come to Kitty Hawk and see for themselves, no one would come. When Guglielmo Marconi revealed that he could send a message through the air without wires, some of his relatives had him sent to a psychiatrist for examination. They were convinced that he had lost his ability to reason.

Contempt prior to examination is a trap that will limit your opportunity, applied faith, enthusiasm, and creativity.

Do not confuse a suspension of belief in something unproved with a certainty that anything new is impossible. Accurate thinking is designed to help you understand new ideas or unusual facts, not to keep you from examining them.

Controlled Habits

I have repeatedly emphasized that your thoughts are the only thing over which you can exert complete control. Because your mind is so subject to the dominating influences in your environment, you must take control over those influences by developing beneficial mental habits. This process is called controlled habits.

The process of controlling your habits is miraculous. It translates the power of thought into action. But if your habits are poor or bad, it can bring misery and failure. Your success depends on the strength and quality of your controlled habits.

Think of your mind as photographic film. Film registers any object reflected on it. It does not select the object it records, and it has no control over the focus of the image or the length of the exposure it receives. You, the photographer, select the image, adjust the lens, manipulate the light and shutter speed. The quality of the picture that is taken depends on your skill in controlling all these elements.

For your mental film, the subject of your composition is your definite major purpose. You frame it as you choose, illuminate it with the fire of your burning obsession, and expose your mind to it for the time that you determine.

Few professional photographers take one shot of an important image. They do over the shot, adjusting all the elements of the process slightly, so that a perfect image is finally recorded. Similarly, instead of a single photo session, you will work on your mental image on a daily basis, repeatedly exposing your brain to the image of your definite major purpose.

This repeated "photographing" of your definite major purpose then becomes a habit, a controlled habit, since you have consciously decided upon the nature of your actions.

The repeated reflection of the light of your burning obsession—which springs from your emotions—will also register this image upon your subconscious, which will work, without your knowledge, to bring the image to fruition by inspiring you, through your imagination, with ideas and plans for attaining your purpose.

The manifestations of these ideas will not simply appear. Your subconscious cannot deposit a new car in your driveway or ten thousand dollars in your bank account. Accurate thinking requires persistent action in applying these ideas and all the principles of success. This is why I have placed such strong emphasis on daily personal initiative in everything you do, for you must also develop the controlled habit of action.

At first action may require every bit of conscious mental control you can exercise. But every time you act, you strengthen that controlled habit, so that the process becomes more ingrained. Your enthusiasm and your applied faith will also drive you. Both these qualities will increase as you make action a controlled habit.

Work will no longer be drudgery; it will become as pleasurable as eating when you are hungry. Strange things that will give you hope and courage will begin happening. People will begin to cooperate with you in a friendlier spirit and without your asking them to do so. Unexpected opportunities for attaining your definite major purpose will spring up around you as the result of your action. Your imagination will become keener and more alert. You will work longer with less fatigue. You will see the world in terms of hope and faith because the controlled habit of action has alerted you to their possibility. With these changes will come improvements in every aspect of your life.

Accurate thinking depends heavily on several other principles of success: definiteness of purpose, self-discipline, prompt decision making, and a positive mental attitude. It also plays an important role in the next principle, controlled attention, which will bring even more focus to your efforts toward your definite major purpose.

◆ 11 ◆

CONTROL YOUR ATTENTION

The Power of Controlled Attention
◆
Controlled Attention and the Other Principles of Success
◆
Controlled Attention and Autosuggestion
◆
Controlled Attention at Work

By adopting a definite major purpose, you have selected an object on which you have to focus your controlled attention. Forget the old saying "Don't put all your eggs in one basket." You have to put all your eggs in one basket and concentrate your attention on protecting that basket and getting it to the market.

Controlled attention is the act of coordinating all the faculties of the mind and directing their combined power to a given end. It is both an outgrowth of many of the other principles of success and an important aid to them.

The Power of Controlled Attention

Concentration upon a single idea has been the hallmark of success for countless people and organizations.

Intel is a manufacturer of computer chips. By concentrating its energy on building better chips, in less than a decade it has more than quadrupled the speed at which computer processors can deal with information. The rate at which it is able to design and introduce even speedier chips grows faster every year. This happens because Intel concentrates its attention on microprocessors and doesn't worry about other things like software or modems.

Donna Karan is a premier designer of women's professional clothing. Her company dresses more female executives than any other. Because Karan doesn't spend her time coming up with a line of designer jeans or swimsuits, she dominates a lucrative market through controlled attention.

Henry Long's paint-manufacturing company, Keeler & Long, concentrates its attention on producing industrial paints. You probably haven't heard of Keeler & Long because it doesn't bother with the sort of paint you use in your home. Instead it makes paint that can withstand a nuclear meltdown or last for years on electrical transformers, and it is recognized as the best paint manufacturer of its kind. Even the White House has been repainted with its product.

Marcel Proust concentrated his attention on a single massive work, *Remembrance of Things Past*, a series of novels that cemented his reputation as one of the major novelists of the twentieth century.

Mother Teresa has concentrated her attention on relieving the suffering of the poor in India. From a single mission she expanded her efforts to more than two hundred sites around the world and won the Nobel Peace Prize. The scope of her plan grew, but she has never wavered in the attention she pays to it.

Whatever your enterprise, concentration on your definite major purpose is essential. It projects a clear picture of your definite purpose upon your conscious mind and holds it there until it is taken over by your subconscious and acted upon.

Controlled Attention and the Other Principles of Success

What I call the Law of Harmonious Attraction means that forces and things which are suited to the needs of one another have a natural tendency to come together.

As you master the principles of success and apply them, you will find that you benefit from the Law of Harmonious Attraction. You will condition your mind so that it will attract only the things you desire, and since you will be eliminating from your mind all conflicting emotions, such as fear, envy, greed, hatred, jealousy, and doubt, you will not be distracted by anything they might attract. Thus you will be in an even better position to control your attention.

Here is how the different principles strengthen and benefit from controlled attention:

Definiteness of Purpose

Deciding on what you want, creating a plan for getting it, and carrying out that plan obviously will require you to concentrate the major portions of your thoughts and efforts toward the attainment of that end. You need an object upon which to concentrate your attention, and once you have selected that object, it will grow closer—and your view of it will grow clearer—the more you concentrate your attention upon it.

The Mastermind Alliance

Forming a mastermind alliance is one of the first effects of controlled attention, since you must do so with care. In turn, the alliance intensifies your concentration by creating a mass psychology which increases your faith, self-reliance, imagination, creative vision, personal initiative, enthusiasm, and will to win. You will keep moving toward your definite major purpose when you are surrounded by others who lend you aid and encouragement, whereas if you work alone, you will be inclined to slow down, become discouraged, and quit.

Applied Faith

When you adopt a definite major purpose and surround yourself with a mastermind group, you demonstrate faith in your ability to attain your objective by persistent endeavor. Your controlled attention has given faith space in which to take root and grow. Likewise, it is much easier to concentrate your attention on something you believe will happen than it is to focus on an event which seems unlikely. Thus the power of your faith is combined with the results of your controlled attention, giving it tremendous power.

Positive Mental Attitude

By the time you have taken the previous basic steps, your mental attitude will already have become predominantly positive. Many of the self-imposed limitations of fear, doubt, and discouragement will have disappeared because you are already seeing evidence of what you can accomplish. You will have no room left in your mind for thoughts of failure. You will be so busy carrying out your definite major purpose that you will have no time for hesitation or procrastination, nor any desire to do either.

Going the Extra Mile

Applying this principle requires continuous action since it must be a part of everything you do. Your concentrated attention in applying it adds momentum to your efforts and inspires enthusiasm and faith in your mastermind allies, as well as in others you encounter. This, in turn, increases your positive mental attitude, making it even easier to control your attention.

Personal Initiative

Applied personal initiative organizes your plans for attaining your definite purpose, then, with the aid of your mastermind allies, tests those plans for soundness. As with going the extra mile, controlled attention to the results of your initiative is crucial, and every positive thing that happens as a result of that initiative strengthens your will and thus your controlled attention.

Self-Discipline

Self-discipline harnesses and controls all emotions, both positive and negative, allowing you to guard against the dissipation of energy through either expressing your negative emotions or neglecting to use your positive ones. Your emotional power is available for the concentration of your attention.

At this point your mind is beginning to function like a well-constructed machine, with no wasted motion and no energy-sapping friction. You have acquired the skill of transmuting your emotions into a powerful driving force for attaining your definite major purpose.

You have also begun to acquire control over your willpower. Your willpower brings all the departments of your mind under complete control and puts them to work in attaining your definite major purpose.

You are now approaching the apex of efficiency in controlled attention.

Creative Vision

Your imagination will already have been greatly stimulated by the previous steps. Your subconscious mind, impressed with the object of your definite purpose, will swing into action on its own, rendering up ideas, plans, and hunches whose clarity and applicability will surprise you.

You will notice new opportunities for attaining your definite major purpose. Friendly forms of cooperation from others will present themselves. Everything you touch will become a tool in your hands to promote your success. Even the laws of averages and luck will operate in your favor.

But don't be mistaken. In back of these lucky breaks is a definite cause that you have brought into being: controlled attention.

Accurate Thinking

Long before you have reached the point of actively cultivating accurate thinking, you will have stopped guessing and started making your plans on the basis of known facts and sound hypotheses. But as your plans begin to take effect, accurate thinking becomes a necessity. Controlled attention hones your thinking, and accurate thinking means that your attention is applied only where it is needed.

Learning from Defeat

When setbacks occur, you will use your controlled attention to find, examine, and nurture the seed of equivalent benefit that comes with every unhappiness. Defeat will be nothing but a signal for greater and more determined effort. It will be fuel to feed the fires of your willpower.

You will also learn to delve into your memory to examine defeats that occurred before you selected your definite major purpose. Controlled attention makes every moment of your life valuable to you.

Enthusiasm

Enthusiasm takes the drudgery out of your work and makes it a labor of love. Your enthusiasm for something automatically leads to your concentrating your attention on it, and it impresses your dominating thoughts on your subconscious.

Controlled attention directs your enthusiasm to definite ends, and the nearer you come to those ends, the more your enthusiasm grows.

Attractive Personality

By developing an attractive personality, you remove much of the opposition you may face from other people and replace it with the cooperation of allies in addition to your mastermind group. Controlled attention helps you improve those elements of your personality that require discipline and gives you the resolve to remove bad habits. In return, your attractive personality provides more opportunity for the use of your controlled attention through increased influence and opportunity.

Mastering these twelve of the Seventeen Principles of Success represents an important step in developing your controlled attention and taking possession of your mind. You come to better understand and influence both your greatest enemy and your greatest friend: yourself.

Controlled Attention and Autosuggestion

The chapter on self-discipline underscores the influence of your daily environment in your struggle for success. One of the most effective ways to shape this environment to your benefit is the process of autosuggestion.

Autosuggestion occurs both consciously and unconsciously. Every thought you have, every word you speak are recorded in your memory, whether those thoughts and words are positive or negative.

The objects on which you deliberately concentrate your attention become the dominating influences in your environment. If your thoughts are fixed on poverty or the physical signs of poverty, these influences are transferred to your subconscious by autosuggestion.

If you continue to concentrate on poverty, you will condition your mind to accept poverty as an unavoidable circumstance, and you will eventually become poverty-conscious. This is how millions of people condemn themselves to lives of poverty.

The principle of autosuggestion works in precisely the same manner when your dominating thoughts are fixed, through controlled attention, upon success and security. This habit leads to the development of a success consciousness.

When you voluntarily fix your attention upon a definite major purpose of a positive nature and force your mind, through daily habits of thought, to dwell on that subject, you condition your subconscious mind to act on that purpose.

Controlled attention, when it is focused on the object of your definite major purpose, is the medium by which you positively apply the principle of autosuggestion. There is no other way to do this.

The difference between controlled and uncontrolled attention is great. You can feed your mind on thoughts which will produce what you desire, or you can neglect your mind, allowing it to feed on thoughts that will produce results you don't desire.

Your mind is never inactive, even in sleep. It constantly reacts to the influences which reach it. The object of controlled attention is to keep your mind busy through thoughts which will be helpful in attaining the object of your desires. If you neglect controlling your attention, your mind will become fixed on negative influences.

Controlled Attention at Work

Chemistry teaches us that individual elements can combine to form new substances that are very different from the components that constitute them. Water is a simple example: Both oxygen and hydrogen are gases, but when two oxygen atoms combine with one hydrogen atom, they form a liquid—and a highly useful one at that. Sodium and chlorine are volatile and dangerous in their pure states, but when one atom of each forms a pair, they become ordinary table salt.

The same is true of thought. Thoughts of one nature can combine with those of another sort, and controlled attention is the means by which you decide the process. If your child is threatened by an oncoming car, fear for his or her safety and love for him or her will combine into thoughts of action, leading you to pull the child out of the way. Both the initial thoughts are strong, but it is the combination of the two that is strongest and most effective at preventing harm.

Observation and experience have taught me that the following principles of success, when combined in your mind, can produce power bordering on the miraculous:

1. Definiteness of purpose
2. Self-discipline through emotional control
3. Autosuggestion applied to attaining your purpose
4. Willpower actively engaged and directed toward your purpose
5. Controlled attention
6. Personal initiative
7. Creative vision
8. Applied faith

Here's an example of these combined principles at work. Suppose you are faced by a common problem: You need a sum of money for a specific purpose, and you need it by a certain date. There are two ways to deal with this. You can worry about it but do nothing to raise the money. Or you can go after it in earnest by combining the above principles.

If you know how much money you need and make up your mind to get it on time, you have definiteness of purpose. When you put your mind to work to devise and carry out a plan for getting the money, and you exclude all other thoughts, you are exhibiting controlled attention, applied through personal initiative.

Your mind is cleared of all fear and doubt. That is self-discipline working through willpower, expressed in applied faith, and acted upon through autosuggestion.

This combination of forces will stimulate the imagination and cause it to create the means through which the money can be procured. Once this happens, of course, it is still up to you to act on that plan to the best of your ability.

You can draw on any of the seventeen principles in this process, although the major ones are listed above. The two constants in any combination must be controlled attention and definiteness of purpose.

Thomas Edison once wrote:

The most important factors of invention can be described in a few words. They consist first of definite knowledge as to what one wishes to achieve [definiteness of purpose, creative vision]. . . . One must fix his mind on that purpose with persistence and begin searching for that which he seeks, making use of all other accumulated knowledge on the subject [master-mind group, controlled attention]. He must keep on searching no matter how many times he may meet with disappointment [willpower]. He must refuse to be influenced by the fact that someone else may have tried the same idea without success [self-discipline, applied faith]. He must keep himself sold on the idea that the solution of his problem exists somewhere, and that he will find it [autosuggestion].

When a man makes up his mind to solve any problem, he may at first meet opposition; but if he holds on and keeps on searching, he will be sure to find some sort of solution. The trouble with most people is that they quit before they start. In all my experiences, I do not recall having ever found the solution to any problem connected with my work on my first attempt. And one of the most surprising things is the fact that when I have discovered the thing for which I am searching, I generally find that it has been within my reach all the time; but nothing except persistence and a will to win would have revealed it.

Such is the power of controlled attention. It harnesses many of the other principles, heightens their power, and, in turn, is increased itself. Are you ready to concentrate your attention on the task at hand?

✦ 12 ✦

INSPIRE TEAMWORK

What Is Teamwork?
✦
Teamwork Turns a Company Around
✦
Teamwork as a Model for Business

Cooperation, like love and friendship, is something you get by giving. There are many travelers on the road that leads to happiness. You will need their cooperation, and they will need yours.

And there will be other generations after ours. Their lot in life will depend largely on the inheritance we leave them. We all must become bridge builders, not only for the present generation but for generations yet unborn.

The spirit of unselfish teamwork will provide greater benefits for both you and your generation as well as help those to come. In building a better world for your children, you will be preparing yourself for the better things in life that come as a result of friendly cooperation.

This kind of cooperation has been a major part of the growth of the United States into the most powerful and economically advantaged nation in the world. As Americans we are bound in a common cause, and no matter what misfortunes overtake us, we must shoulder those burdens equally in the spirit of unselfish teamwork if we are to retain our preeminence.

Until we become inspired with the spirit of teamwork and recognize the oneness of all people and the fellowship of all humanity, we will not truly benefit from the principle of co-operative effort. Greed and selfishness have no part in this spirit.

In this chapter you will see examples of the power of co-operation at work and learn how to inspire it in the people you work with.

What Is Teamwork?

In your mastermind alliance you build a small group of individuals committed to the same definite purpose. You all share the same burning obsession, you each benefit from the increased enthusiasm, imagination, and knowledge, and you are in agreement on the division of the rewards of your labor. Teamwork establishes much the same relation-ship, but since it involves working with people who proba-bly don't have the same burning obsession you do, it requires more effort on your part to maintain a commit-ment to the work you seek from others and for them to dis-cover their own desires.

Management guru Peter Drucker says that all employees "have to see themselves as executives," so that they see the work they do in the context of an entire operation. Managers must learn to subordinate themselves to the work they are doing and not become concerned with promoting their own positions at the expense of their employees. Drucker recalls the example of General Douglas MacArthur, who started ev-ery staff meeting with a presentation from the most junior of-ficer present. MacArthur allowed no one to interrupt because he knew it was important to build the confidence of his offi-cers. He wanted and needed that confidence.

Your habit of going the extra mile must extend to your associates. Even if your benefits are generous and your salaries good, people can come to take these things for granted. You should anticipate your associates' needs and act before they even recognize them.

Teamwork sometimes appears among people who are forced by necessity to work together, but it is undependable and never lasts. The United States and the Soviet Union were allies against Hitler, but the alliance evaporated as soon as he was vanquished.

True teamwork depends on relating yourself to others in such a way that they work with you willingly. It is up to you to supply the motives for that willingness and to be alert to any changes in it. Teamwork is a never-ending process, and even though it depends on everyone involved, the responsibility for it lies with you.

Teamwork Turns a Company Around

During its early years National Cash Register found itself in financial difficulty because a negative attitude had set in among its sales representatives. Hugh Chalmers, the company's sales manager, called his reps together to address this problem.

Chalmers realized that the sales reps were the company's greatest asset, which could be preserved only by restoring the fullest measure of teamwork.

When the reps were assembled, Chalmers stood up in front of them and said, "Some of our competitors have started a whispering campaign that this company is in such financial difficulty that we will not be able to pull through; there are rumors that we intend to cut our sales force and lay many of you off. This simply is not true.

"Some of you have been influenced by these reports until your sales have dropped off alarmingly. I've brought you here to give you an opportunity to speak for yourselves. I hope you will speak frankly, no matter how you feel.

"The meeting is now open to you. Will each of you please tell what has happened to curtail your sales and what you think we should do to restore that old team spirit which existed before these rumors were spread?"

One of the reps stood up. "My sales have been dropping off because I have a territory that has been hit hard by drought. Nobody is buying cash registers because their business has suffered. Worse, our competitors are cutting prices and offering deals which make it impossible for me to compete with them.

"And," the rep continued, "this is a presidential election year and everyone in my territory is worried about the outcome. No one seems to be interested in buying anything until they know what will be happening in Washington next year."

A second rep stood up. His story was even more negative than the first one, full of woe and an evident conviction that the company was doomed. He announced boldly that he was looking for another job.

Before he finished, Chalmers jumped up and held out his hand for silence, then exclaimed, "This meeting will take a fifteen-minute recess while I get my shoes shined. Please remain seated."

And to the astonishment of the sales force Chalmers sent for the young boy who shined shoes in the company's factory, a common service in those days. Paying no attention to his audience, Chalmers chatted with the boy.

At the end of the conversation Chalmers handed the boy a dime and then announced that the youngster was going to make a speech.

No one could have been more surprised than the shoeshine boy. "I don't know how to make a speech," he protested.

"Yes, you do," Chalmers replied. "And you can make a better one than the last two we heard. I'll help you.

"How old are you?" Chalmers asked.

"Eleven," the boy replied.

"How long have you been shining shoes in this plant?"

"Six months."

"Good! How much do you get for shining shoes?"

"I get a nickel," the boy replied, "but sometimes I get another for tips, like you gave me."

"Who had your job before you did?"

"It was a boy named Ted."

"And how old was he?" Chalmers queried.

"Seventeen."

"Do you know why he left?"

"I heard he thought he couldn't make a living."

"Can you make a living at a nickel a shine?" Chalmers asked.

"Oh, yes, sir. I give my mother ten dollars on Friday, and I put five dollars in the bank, and I have two dollars left for spending money. Some weeks I make more than that. I'm saving on the side to buy a bicycle, but my mother doesn't know anything about that."

"Thank you," Chalmers said. "You have made a very fine speech."

Turning to his audience, Chalmers said, "You have heard this boy's story. Now let me tell you want it means.

"In the first place, I want to call your attention to the fact that this boy is doing a job that used to be held by someone six years older than he, doing the same work, charging the same price, and serving the same people who work in this plant.

"The older boy quit this job because he couldn't make a living from it, but this boy not only has money for himself and his dreams but helps support his family. He is working the same territory the older boy worked, but he is working it in a different mental attitude.

"He is cooperative; he goes about his work with a smile on his face; he expects success, and he is finding it. The older boy was indifferent, moody, and never took the trouble to say 'thank you' when his patrons handed him a nickel. Therefore, that was all they did hand him; no tips, no great amount of repeat orders for his services. Of course, he couldn't make a living. Furthermore—"

At this point Chalmers was interrupted by a rep. "I get the point! Those of us who have been failing in the field have been buying other people's hard-luck stories instead of selling them cash registers. I know that is what I've been doing. I've been trying to do my job with a negative mind, and that's why my sales have fallen off. I don't know how anyone else feels about it, but I'm going back to my territory and start working it as I never worked it before. I can promise you that in the future you will get orders for cash registers from me instead of hard luck stories."

Another rep jumped up and cried, "That goes for me, too!" Then another. Soon pandemonium broke out with everyone talking at the same time. The conference wound up that night with a banquet at which every sales rep promised to return to the field with a new spirit of faith.

The year that followed was one of the most profitable in the history of NCR. What happened? A leader had seen what it was his workers needed. In this case it was a kick in the pants that showed them that success is something you create for yourself, not something others steal from you. Chalmers refired their dedication to their tasks with a vivid example of the success that was available to anyone committed to its pursuit.

Although he strongly suspected what ailed his reps, he was wise enough to give them the opportunity to express their concerns; Chalmers knew he needed a frank working relationship with his force. He didn't punish those who had the courage to speak up. He offered every one of them, complainer or not, the same thing: a vision of what he could accomplish. And he started his speech with the reassurance that the company was standing behind its sales force.

Chalmers maintained a positive attitude in his relations with his reps, and he influenced them to respond in kind:

Teamwork costs so little in time and effort, and it pays huge dividends. One wonders why so many people go out of their way to make life miserable for themselves and others by failing to realize this.

Teamwork as a Model for Business

Years ago an article by Robert Littell in *Reader's Digest* described a management system in use by the McCormick spice company in Baltimore. This system was revolutionary in its time, though more and more companies have now adopted something similar. McCormick called it "the multiple management plan," which is just another way of saying "teamwork."

When Charles P. McCormick succeeded his uncle as head of the company, he decided to share the responsibilities of running the show with those who could be taught to take it. He picked seventeen young people from the company's front office and made them the Junior Board of Directors. They were charged with examining and discussing everything the company did, then presenting their findings to the regular board—as long as they were unanimous in their decision.

As Littell wrote, "A flood of energy and new ideas was released. Men who had felt themselves to be merely glorified clerks tasted responsibility and clamored for more. Even in the first year and a half practically all of the Juniors' recommendations were adopted."

The same policy was applied to the assembly line, where a Factory Board was formed with the same charge. The three boards met together weekly in a spirit of harmony, everyone seeking ways to improve business and efficiency, to raise McCormick another notch higher.

McCormick's personnel policy was truly forward-thinking. Dismissing a worker required the signatures of four superiors who thought the action was necessary, and anyone threatened with dismissal was allowed to plead his or her case. As Littell noted, "McCormick & Company charges itself with an error if it lets a man go until he has been helped to see that his going is just and necessary. . . ."

The multiple management plan worked for McCormick & Company because of the spirit of human understanding and teamwork the individual workers put into it—a spirit which began with management and was readily embraced by the employees. And obviously this spirit of understanding and teamwork served to provide sound economies in the management of the company because it recognized and appropriately awarded merit, down to the humblest employee, and at the same time eliminated the unwilling and unfit from the organization.

People will work harder for personal recognition and a word of commendation where it is deserved than they will for money alone. No one wants to feel as if he or she is merely a cog in a wheel. Your job as a leader is to see that everyone has a role in your group or organization and that he or she recognizes the importance of that role.

Through the multiple management plan McCormick put the soul back into its firm and provided every worker with a very real desire and worthwhile motive to go the extra mile and to do it with a positive mental attitude. That is the essence of teamwork.

There is no record of anyone's ever having made a great contribution to civilization without the cooperation of others. Even great artists like Michelangelo depended upon assistants, craftsmen, and patrons to make their work possible.

There is a state of mind that tends to make people akin, establishes rapport between minds, and provides the power of attraction that gains the friendly teamwork of others. This state of mind, like so many of the other priceless assets of life, is usually attained by the concentration of the mind on attaining a definite major purpose backed by an appropriate motive and self-discipline.

That state is enthusiasm. It is contagious. Infect others with your enthusiasm, and teamwork will be the inevitable result.

◆ 13 ◆
LEARN FROM ADVERSITY
AND DEFEAT

Everyone Faces Defeat
◆
Adversity Becomes a Blessing
◆
The Major Causes of Personal Failure
◆
The Benefits of Defeat
◆
Your Attitude Toward Defeat

Throughout this book I've reminded you to look for the seed of an equivalent benefit in every defeat you experience. This isn't always easy when you've suffered a setback, but it is an important part of the science of personal achievement. The time to begin mastering this skill is now, instead of while you're licking your wounds.

Failure and pain are one language through which nature speaks to every living creature, pointing out mistakes. Animals may become timid so that they avoid a threatening situation when it arises again; you must become humble so that you can acquire wisdom and understanding. Realize that the turning point at which you begin to attain success is usually defined by some form of defeat or failure.

With this realization, you need not accept defeat as failure but only as a temporary event that may prove to be a blessing in disguise.

Everyone Faces Defeat

No one who has attained success has not met with some form of failure comparable with the scope of his or her success. Edison "failed" with more than ten thousand different attempts to create a lightbulb before he hit on the formula that worked. Jonas Salk tried countless different media to cultivate the polio virus for a vaccine before he discovered that monkey brain tissue did the job.

Debbie Fields founded the high-profile Mrs. Fields Cookies chain with a single store and expanded it worldwide very quickly. Too quickly, in fact. The costs of expansion crippled the company, and Fields found herself deeply in debt. She learned that trying to own and run all the stores was simply too much. Now she franchises operations instead of running them herself, and the company is profitable and growing once more.

Defeat should be accepted merely as a test which permits you to discover the nature of your thoughts and their relation to your definite major purpose. Knowing this modifies your reaction to adversity and keeps you striving toward your goal. Defeat is never the same as failure unless and until it has been accepted as such. Emerson said:

> Our strength grows out of our weakness. Not until we are pricked and stung and sorely shot at, awakens the indignation which arms itself with secret forces. A great man is always willing to be little. While he sits on the cushion of advantages he goes to sleep. When he is pushed, tormented, defeated, he has a chance to learn something; he has been put on his wits; on his manhood; he has gained facts; learned from his ignorance; been cured of the insanity of conceit; has got moderation and real skill.

Defeat, however, does not promise the full-blown flower of benefit, only the seed from which some benefit may be coaxed. You must recognize the seed, nurture, and cultivate it by definiteness of purpose; otherwise it will never sprout. Nature looks with disfavor on any attempt to obtain something for nothing.

You need to thank your faults when they are revealed to you because you cannot truly understand them until you have fought them.

Adversity Becomes a Blessing

Milo C. Jones operated a small farm in Wisconsin. He was barely subsisting at it when disaster struck: He suffered a paralyzing stroke.

His relatives were so convinced that he was a hopeless invalid that they put him to bed and left him there. Unable to use his body, Jones turned to his mind. Almost immediately he had an idea that was destined to compensate him for his misfortune.

He summoned his relatives together and charged them with planting his entire acreage with corn. That corn would be used to feed a herd of pigs. Those pigs would be slaughtered and turned into sausage.

Within a few years Jones's sausage was being sold in stores all across the nation. You know it as Jones Farm sausage. Milo Jones and his family became wealthier than they had ever dreamed.

This happened because Jones was forced by adversity to turn to a resource he had never really used: his mind. He formed a definite major purpose and a plan for realizing it. He created a mastermind alliance with his family, and with applied faith they carried out the plan that a stroke had brought to a poor farmer.

When defeat overtakes you, don't spend your time counting your losses. Save it to count your gains and assets, and you will realize that they are greater than any loss you have suffered.

You may wonder why Milo C. Jones had to be overcome by a debilitating ailment before he discovered the power of his mind. Others might say that his compensation for that ailment was only financial and therefore not equivalent to his loss of mobility.

But Jones also received spiritual benefits in realizing the power of his mind and the strength of his family. His success, to be sure, did not restore control of his body. But it did give him control of his destiny, which is the highest form of personal achievement. He could have lived out his life in his bed, worrying about himself and his family. Instead he was able to bring them security they would otherwise never have known.

Prolonged illness, like any crippling defeat, often forces us to stop, look, and listen. We learn to understand that still, small voice which speaks to us from within and leads us to take inventory of the factors which have led to defeat and failure in the past.

Again Emerson points the way in these matters:

A fever, a mutilation, a cruel disappointment, a loss of wealth, a loss of friends, seems [sic] at the moment unpaid loss, and unpayable. But the sure years reveal the deep remedial force that underlies all facts. The death of a dear friend, spouse, brother, lover, which seemed nothing but privation somewhat later assumes the aspect of a guide or genius; for it commonly operates revolutions in our way of life, terminates an epoch of infancy or of youth which was waiting to be closed, breaks up a wonted occupation, or a household, or style of living, allows the formation of new ones more friendly to the growth of character.

It permits or constrains the formation of new acquaintances, and the reception of new influences that prove of first importance to the next years; and the man or woman who would have remained a sunny garden flower, with no room for its roots and too much sunshine for its head, by the falling of the walls and the neglect of the gardener is made the banyan of the forest, yielding shade and fruit to wide neighborhoods of man.

Time is relentless in preserving the seed of an equivalent benefit that hides within a defeat. The best time to begin looking for that seed in a new defeat is now. But you can also examine past losses for the seeds they contain. Indeed, sometimes the weight of the loss prevents you from searching at the time. But now, with your increased wisdom and experience, you are ready to examine any loss for the lesson it can teach you.

The Major Causes of Personal Failure

To give you some perspective on the losses you face, I have below listed the most common and powerful causes of failure. When you recognize any that have hampered you, it is important that you do not berate yourself for their presence in your life. Instead you must resolve to do something about them, and do it now!

1. The habit of drifting through life without a definite major purpose
2. Meddlesome curiosity about other people's affairs
3. Inadequate education
4. Lack of self-discipline, manifested as both uncontrolled appetites and indifference to opportunity
5. Lack of ambition
6. Ill health that results from negative thinking and poor diet
7. Unfavorable childhood influences
8. Lack of persistence and follow-through
9. Negative mental attitude
10. Lack of emotional control
11. The desire to get something for nothing

12. Failure to reach decisions promptly and firmly when all the facts needed for the decision are available
13. One or more of the seven basic fears: poverty, criticism, ill health, loss of love, old age, loss of liberty, death
14. Poor selection of a spouse
15. Overcaution or the lack of caution
16. Poor choice of a vocation or occupation
17. Indiscriminate spending of time and money
18. Lack of control over the tongue
19. Intolerance
20. Failure to cooperate with others in a spirit of harmony
21. Disloyalty
22. Lack of vision and imagination
23. Egotism and vanity
24. Desire for revenge
25. Unwillingness to go the extra mile

That's quite a list. But the causes of failure are many, and often you will find more than just one has led to your downfall.

In my youth I founded a magazine in Chicago dedicated to exhorting readers to strive for success. I lacked the capital for this venture, so I entered into a partnership with my printer. The magazine was a success, and even though I had to work long, endless hours, I was happy.

But I was not paying attention. My success threatened another publisher, and without my knowledge he bought out my printer partner and took over my magazine. I was out of work and separated from my labor of love in a most humiliating way.

Many of the above causes for failure were responsible for my defeat. The most important was that I had neglected to cooperate with my partner in a spirit of harmony; I bickered with him often about trivial details of publication. When the opportunity came to be free of me—and to make a profit doing it—he jumped at the chance. My egotism and vanity were responsible for much of this, as were my general lack of caution in business affairs and my sharp tongue.

But—and this is an important "but"—I did manage to find the seed of equivalent benefit by seeing these flaws in my way of doing business. I left Chicago for New York, where I founded a new magazine, one over which I retained control. To achieve this end, I truly had to inspire cooperation in my new business partners, who were risking their money without the power my former partner had kept. I also had to be much more cautious in my business planning since I depended more deeply on my own resources.

The result was a magazine that, within a year, had more than twice the circulation of my previous venture. And it was as a part of my efforts to build the profits of that magazine that I conceived a series of correspondence courses which were the first codification of the science of personal achievement.

I stood at a fork in the road when I was dethroned from my Chicago magazine. I could have given up and returned to the quiet lawyer's job my wife's family urged on me. Instead I recognized the seeds of equivalent benefit in my defeat, and I nurtured that seed beyond my wildest dreams.

The Benefits of Defeat

- Defeat reveals and breaks bad habits, releasing your energies for a fresh start with better habits.
- Defeat supplants vanity and arrogance with humility, paving the way for more harmonious relationships.
- Defeat causes you to take inventory of your assets and liabilities, both physical and spiritual.
- Defeat strengthens your willpower by providing it with a challenge to greater effort.

Bodybuilders know that it isn't enough just to jerk the barbell up; it has to be returned to its original position twice as slowly as it was raised. This principle is known as resistance training; it requires more control and effort than the showy work of actually lifting the weight.

Defeat can be your resistance training. Every time you return to where you started, do it deliberately, concentrating on the process, so that you train yourself to make even stronger and more powerful progress the next time.

Your Attitude Toward Defeat

Again and again I've stressed that your attitude toward defeat is crucial to mastering it. You can see it only as a loss or as a chance for gain.

The negative attitude toward defeat is effectively summarized by Shakespeare in *Julius Caesar* when the murderer Brutus says:

There is a tide in the affairs of men,
Which taken at the flood, leads on to fortune;
Omitted, all the voyage of their life
Is bound in shallows and in miseries.
On such a full sea are we now afloat;
And we must take the current when it serves,
Or lose our ventures.

These are the words of a doomed man, a man who seals his doom by failing to recognize that there is never just one chance, never just one tide that leads on to fortune.

The positive attitude is very different. Consider this poem by Walter Malone, entitled "Opportunity":

They do me wrong who say I come no more,
When once I knock and fail to find you in;
For every day I stand outside your door,
And bid you wake and rise, to fight and win.

Wail not for precious chances passed away;
Weep not for golden ages on the wane;
Each night I burn the records of the day;
At sunrise every soul is born again.

Laugh like a boy at splendors that have sped,
To vanished joys be blind and deaf and dumb;
My judgments seal the dead past with its dead,
But never bind a moment yet to come.

Malone's vision of defeat is the one you will prefer when
you have discovered that every defeat carries the seed of an
equivalent benefit. Remember, "At sunrise every soul is born
again." That rebirth is the opportunity to put defeat behind
you.

Fear, self-limitation, and the acceptance of your defeat as
final will cause you to be "bound in shallows and in miseries," as Shakespeare suggests. But these things can be overcome by applied faith, a positive mental attitude, and a
definite major purpose.

If you accept defeat as an inspiration to try again with renewed confidence and determination, attaining success will
be only a matter of time. The secret to this is your positive
mental attitude.

Remember, a positive mental attitude attracts success. You
need that attraction most when coping with defeat. Redouble
your efforts to maintain and build your PMA when adversity
strikes, and use your applied faith in yourself and your purpose to put your PMA into action. That is the fundamental
lesson in learning from adversity and defeat.

• 14 •
CULTIVATE CREATIVE
VISION

Synthetic Imagination
✦
Creative Imagination
✦
Creative Vision Goes Beyond Imagination
✦
Creative Vision Is Needed Today

Creative vision requires you to stimulate your imagination to work toward your definite major purpose and to put the results of that imagination to work.

Expressed by people unafraid of criticism, creative vision is responsible for the shape of civilization today. It has brought every advancement in thought, science, and mechanics that allows our current standard of living. It inspires you to pioneer and experiment with new ideas in every field. It is always on the lookout for better ways of doing things.

Creative vision belongs only to people who have the habit of going the extra mile, for it recognizes no nine-to-five working hours and it isn't concerned with monetary rewards. Its aim is doing the impossible.

This chapter will give you great examples of creative vision and show you how to understand the process by which it works so that you can apply it in your own life.

Synthetic Imagination

Imagination, like reasoning, takes two forms: synthetic and creative imagination. Each can contribute to the betterment of your own life and the world around you through creative vision.

Synthetic imagination combines previously recognized ideas, concepts, plans, or facts in a new way or puts them to new use.

An excellent example of synthetic imagination is Edison's invention of the lightbulb. He began with one recognized fact that other people had discovered: A wire could be heated by electricity until it produced light. The problem was that the intense heat quickly burned the wire out. The light never lasted more than a few minutes.

Edison failed more than ten thousand times in his attempt to control this heat. When he found the method, it was by applying another common fact which had simply eluded everyone else. He realized that charcoal is produced by setting wood on fire, covering it with soil, and allowing the fire to smolder until the wood is charred. The soil permits only enough air to reach the fire to keep it burning without blazing.

When Edison recognized this fact, his imagination immediately associated it with the idea of heating the wire. He placed the wire inside a bottle, pumped out most of the air, and produced the first incandescent light. It burned for eight and a half hours.

Edison's creative vision depended on several important principles of the science of personal achievement. He applied the habit of going the extra mile because he labored without immediate pay. He worked with definiteness of purpose and was inspired by applied faith to carry on with his work through an incredible number of failures that would have broken most people.

Finally he applied the mastermind principle by assembling a team of skilled chemists and mechanics to perfect his invention, finding the right kind and thickness of wire, the right quantity of air to leave in the bulb, the best way to construct the bulb, so that his invention took on the most efficient form possible.

Synthetic imagination does not depend on having tremendous personal advantages. Edison had spent only three months in grade school, had supported himself for many years as a telegrapher, and was fired from almost every job he held. He began to lose his hearing early on and eventually became almost completely deaf. But he turned his life around through definiteness of purpose, the habit of going the extra mile, and applied faith.

Thomas Stemberg was a successful executive in the grocery business. Working with a Connecticut-based chain, he opened a string of high-volume megasupermarkets that offered consumers huge selections at low prices.

The stores were very successful, and Stemberg was building a sterling reputation in his business. But he wasn't satisfied. He saw the prosperous grocery megastores and wondered if the megastore concept couldn't be applied to something else.

He wanted to start a large business in a big market underserved by modern distribution methods, offering customers a good value. He formed a mastermind alliance with Leo Kahn, the man who had pioneered the grocery megastores, and in 1986 he opened Staples, the first mega–business-supply store.

Stemberg's idea was so smart, so right that it immediately inspired competitors like Office Depot and OfficeMax, to revolutionize the business supply industry. Despite the competition, Staples surpassed even Stemberg's ambitious expectations. In just seven years sales exceeded one billion dollars.

Thomas Stemberg didn't invent the superstore idea, but he

applied it to a market that had been quiet and humdrum for decades. He developed a definite plan for attaining his goal; he formed a mastermind alliance with Kahn, the man who understood the concept best; he put his plan into action with applied faith; and he went the extra mile by offering customers more and better service than they could get anywhere else.

Synthetic imagination puts the entire sum of human knowledge at your disposal, but like any other part of the science of success, it requires your dedication to making your vision into reality.

Creative Imagination

Creative imagination has its base in the subconscious. It is the medium through which you recognize new ideas and newly learned facts. All your efforts to impress your definite major purpose on your subconscious work to stimulate your creative imagination.

F. W. Woolworth was working as a clerk in a hardware store. He was, at that point, simply determined to be a good and valuable employee. When his boss complained about piles of out-of-date goods that weren't selling, Woolworth's imagination went to work.

"I can sell those items," he told his boss, and with his employer's permission, he set up a table in the store, laid out all of the dud merchandise, and priced everything at ten cents. The stock sold remarkably fast, and soon the owner was searching for anything he could lay his hands on to put on that table, which became the most profitable spot in the store.

Woolworth had the faith to apply his new idea to an entire store; his boss didn't. The Woolworth chain of five-and-dimes quickly spread across the nation, earning him a fortune. His former boss once commented, "Every word I used in turning that man's offer down has cost me about a million dollars I might have earned."

Woolworth was so committed to his then-modest purpose of being a valuable employee that his imagination was ready to back up his commitment with powerful ideas. He certainly went the extra mile for his boss, but because that man didn't have the vision that Woolworth had, other investors formed Woolworth's mastermind alliance and profited from it.

Creative Vision Goes Beyond Imagination

Creative vision is more than an interest in material things; it is a commitment to a better future. Synthetic imagination springs from experience and reason; creative imagination springs from your commitment to your definite purpose. Creative vision depends heavily upon creative imagination, but it is also more than that.

Imagination recognizes limitations, handicaps, and opposition; creative vision rides over these as if they did not exist, for it has its base in Infinite Intelligence.

One of the purest examples I know of creative vision is illustrated by the story of Dr. Elmer Gates. Gates was an inventor who worked at the same time as Edison, but his methods and background were very different. He was a highly trained scientist, and his patents actually outnumbered Edison's two to one.

Gates applied creative vision in a remarkably simple process. He would enter a soundproof room, sit down at a table with pencil and paper, and turn off the lights. He then concentrated his thoughts on a particular problem and waited for the ideas that he needed for its solution.

Sometimes ideas flowed to Gates immediately; sometimes he had to wait for as much as an hour before they came. Occasionally nothing happened. At other times he perceived solutions to other problems that he hadn't even been thinking about.

Dr. Gates's creative vision transcended imagination because he had developed it into a faculty he could call upon at will. Creative vision produces results, not alibis.

Creative Vision Is Needed Today

There are countless calls for creative vision in the world today.

- We need forms of energy that do not pollute or drain our environment.
- We need schools that capture the attention of our young people and teach them to better themselves.
- We need cures and vaccines for terrible diseases that threaten the earth's people.
- We need people who can show small business how to use and profit from rapidly changing technology.
- We need plans for controlling the cost of health care and making it affordable for every honest worker without destroying the incentive of the professionals who provide it.

There is both challenge and opportunity in these needs, and I raise them only to start you thinking about the scope of the possibilities for creative vision.

There is a place in America for every person who can render any type of useful service and is willing to render it with the right mental attitude. If you have creative vision, you will recognize this and profit from it. You will never complain of a lack of opportunity.

Great leaders of every generation in this country began their careers in humble occupations. Andrew Carnegie was a bobbin boy in a textile mill. W. Clement Stone was a newsboy. Harry Truman was a haberdasher. Ruth Bader Ginsburg had to become a law secretary when she graduated from law school because judges couldn't imagine hiring a woman clerk, yet now she sits on the Supreme Court.

It makes little difference where you begin. The important thing to ask is: Where are you going? What motive inspires you to give your best? Are you willing to go the extra mile? Are you a clock-watcher, eager for the day to end? Or do you look for the opportunity to make yourself indispensable to others?

These are the questions you must ask yourself. If you have creative vision, you can answer them. You know where you are going, you know what you desire, and you know that life never lets you get something for nothing without eventually forcing you to pay more for it than it is worth.

When you have creative vision, you know that you can succeed only by helping others to succeed, and you know that it isn't necessary for anyone to fail in the process.

Creative vision lets you make decisions quickly. And it lets you change those decisions as soon as you realize a mistake has been made. It frees you from fear of others, for it makes you feel at peace with yourself in your knowledge that you are fair and honest.

It's a common human trait to envy people who have attained success, looking at them only in the moments of their triumph and forgetting the prices they had to pay. Often we suspect that they owe their success to some sort of pull, luck, or dishonesty.

But creative vision makes you keenly aware of the price of personal achievement because you yourself know its labors. You understand the benefits of sharing your blessings, experiences, and opportunities with others; you know that your success actually depends on it.

If you feel the need for a creative vision in your life, you can begin to develop it by getting on better terms with your own conscience, inspiring yourself with greater self-reliance, providing yourself with a definite major purpose, and keeping your mind so busy with that purpose that you have no time left for fear and doubt.

Nothing will happen in your life that you do not inspire by your own initiative. Creative vision is the power which inspires the development of that personal initiative.

◆ 15 ◆
MAINTAIN
SOUND HEALTH

The Rhythms of Life
◆
The Influence of Your Mind
◆
Essentials of Success and Happiness
◆
The Force of Fear
◆
The Force of a Positive Mental Attitude
◆
Eating Habits
◆
Rhythms in Relaxation
◆
Sleep
◆
Exercise
◆
Sex and Sublimation
◆
Effective Mind-Body Stimulants

You want to get the greatest vigor and fullest use from your body. You can do this if you understand two important points:

1. Your body and mind are one, effectively a mind-body.
2. Your mind-body is, in turn, at one with nature.

The health of your mind and body cannot be separated. Anything that affects the soundness of your mind will affect your body, and anything that affects your body will touch your mind. This is why I refer to you as a mind-body.

But you are also affected by your environment, subject to natural laws that govern your mind-body just as much as they affect trees, mountains, birds, and beasts.

Understanding the way in which you can maintain a sound mind-body depends, therefore, on understanding the way nature works. You must learn to work with natural forces, not fight them.

The Rhythms of Life

When you consider the waves of the ocean, the passing of the seasons, the waxing and waning of the moon, you will see that nature moves in rhythms. There is even a rhythm in your own life from birth through childhood and adolescence to full maturity, old age, and finally birth of a new generation. Light, energy, and matter are made up of waves, either moving out in their own rhythm or bound, like a neutron, around the fixed point of the nucleus of the atom.

Nothing about life is static. Movement is constant and rhythmic (though sometimes that rhythm is too large or small for us to perceive immediately). This is one reason why we enjoy music, for it reflects the rhythms and waves of our experience. You must learn to bend and sway with the rhythms of life, not to stand fixed and immobile against them. A sandy beach moves and changes with the rhythms of the waves and lasts for eons; a breakwater is soon destroyed.

Take a look at your life. Is it rhythmical? Are you follow-ing work with play, mental effort with physical effort, eating with fasting, seriousness with humor, sex with transmutation of sex into creative effort?

Your subconscious does its best work on your behalf while your conscious mind is at rest. True inspiration most often comes after your subconscious has been given a task and while your conscious mind is then occupied elsewhere—that is, while your mind is playing.

Archimedes had struggled with the complex problem of determining the relative mass of two objects without finding a solution. It was only when he decided to relax and slip into his bath that his subconscious was stimulated by the water he displaced in his tub. He sprang from his bath with that now-famous cry of "Eureka!" and the solution he had been seeking. Are you giving your mind a chance to relax by play-ing?

Interference with normal rhythmical patterns produces so many problems. If you don't give your mind a rhythm of work and relaxation, your body will be so constantly stimu-lated that you will likely end up with a stress-related disor-der. And without highs and lows, the things that you value begin to pale. Your past failures are what makes success sweet.

You don't really want continuous happiness, for then your happiness would seem dull. One of the major goals of mar-riage counseling is getting couples to understand that there is no such thing as being constantly in love. People in love have a series of loves, like waves on the oceans. In the troughs they are neutral in their feelings, but troughs make the peaks of the waves so much more poignant. As in life, not all the ocean's waves are of the same intensity; there are a few for each of us that reach great heights, and it is the memory and exhilaration of these moments that we store up to call upon when the going gets difficult.

You have to learn to understand the waves and rhythms in

your life and to live within those rhythms in order to be in harmony with the world.

The Influence of Your Mind

Just as you have to understand nature as a complex whole, moving with its own rhythms, you have to understand that your mind and body are a whole, each influencing the other.

Humans are the only thinking creatures, and this power allows you to modify your world and to learn its laws. You need only to conceive the idea and believe in it to achieve the idea.

This is the story of all the successful people who have changed the path of civilization. It took countless hundreds of millions of years for evolution to develop from all the animals that walked or swam a bird that could fly. Yet the Wright brothers, with childlike faith in their own idea, had human beings airborne in a mere twenty years. That is the power of the mind, demonstrated to us by experience and reinforced by the words of countless prophets in touch with Infinite Intelligence. Christ himself said, "All things are possible even unto the end of the world."

Your mind has the higher function in your mind-body. Your body is an exquisitely functioning machine for carrying your mind about and executing the dictates of this powerhouse. A smoothly functioning mind is necessary to a smoothly functioning body.

Some people have bodies that are limited. They can move, see, or speak only with difficulty or not at all. Yet the power of their minds allows them to live full creative lives. Helen Keller is a marvelous example, as are Beethoven and Edison, both of whom suffered from severely impaired hearing. Franklin Roosevelt was barely able to stand on his own, yet he inspired and led our country through the greatest depression and war we ever faced. Senator Bob Dole's arm was permanently injured in World War II, but that has not stopped him from becoming one of our most influential political leaders.

The story of civilization is punctuated with greatness achieved by individuals in spite of physical limitations because these people possessed smoothly functioning minds. On the wings of a definite major purpose, faith, enthusiasm, and a positive mental attitude, they rose farther and farther from any despair over their limitations toward great heights of brilliant achievement. That is the influence of the mind.

Essentials of Success and Happiness

Many of the essential principles of success are also essential to a smoothly functioning mind. A definite major purpose and a plan for carrying it out keep you from vacillating in your efforts. Think of a situation in which you were part of a smoothly functioning plan. You were content with the way the situation was handled. You felt at ease and comfortable. Your mind is always satisfied with the harmony produced by a well-organized plan. Anxiety develops from a poorly organized plan.

Controlled attention, self-discipline, accurate thinking, personal initiative, learning from defeat, and going the extra mile all are mental tools you can use to organize and carry out your plan. They give you satisfaction both in the achievement of each step of your plan and in your overall progress. Satisfactions are important foods for a healthy mind.

Probably the most important single quality for sound mental health is a positive mental attitude and all that it entails. Two of the greatest destructive forces in the human mind are fear and its close partner, anxiety. They kill enthusiasm, destroy faith, blind vision, blunt creative effort, and dispel har-

mony and peace of mind—all qualities necessary for a
positive mental attitude and sound mental health.

The Force of Fear

Fear and anxiety produce unharmonious, irritated restless-
ness in your mind that leads to serious mental maladjust-
ment and produces its counterpart in the body in the form of
serious disease, perhaps even death. There is a growing
awareness in the healing professions that many human ailments are either the product of mental distress or greatly ex-
acerbated by it.

The list of diseases that are brought on by stress is long,
varied, and growing: allergies, asthma, skin disease, hyper-
tension, cardiac problems, arthritis, colitis, and immune dis-
orders.

Some hayfever sufferers start sneezing and itching at the
sight of goldenrod in a vase. Tell them the plant is artificial,
and their symptoms clear. This is a simple example of how
the mind can affect the body negatively.

You must replace fear with understanding and faith in
yourself. To do this, let's look at how fear affects the mech-
anisms of your body.

Temporary, fleeting fear is a normal and important function. It gets you to move out of the way of an oncoming train
or keeps you from walking too near a cliff by momentarily
focusing your attention—your mind—on a problem. Once
the problem is over, this kind of fear is forgotten.

Fear also focuses your bodily functions on a threat. That
old story of a cave dweller frightened by a sound in the
night is a good illustration. Instantaneously the heart begins
pumping faster; blood is diverted from the digestion for use
by the muscles; the blood vessels serving the muscles dilate
to handle increased volume, while those near the skin contract so that less blood is lost in case of a cut. Hearing becomes more acute; the pupils dilate to take in more light; the

adrenaline gland unleashes a torrent of stimulant to provide strength for a fight.

All this is preparation for surviving a battle or chase. The ensuing battle uses up the adrenaline and exhausts the other bodily systems so that they step down from their heightened readiness. Blood leaves the muscles to return to digestive and other functions.

This is an extremely powerful response, one that kept our species alive over millions of years. But it is not intended to be a constant state, for it diverts the body from its normal functions. Still, some of us activate this response to some extent daily or even continually because we live in frequent fear.

You must work to eliminate the causes of those fears.

The fear of the loss of money: Have you set up a system to conserve and develop your assets?

The fear of ill health: Have you sought and followed worthwhile counsel?

The fear of loss of love: Have you put as much effort into increasing your beloved's affection as you would into cultivating an important business prospect?

The fear of death: Have you sought help and understanding to the point where fear is replaced by faith?

The list of fears is endless, yet to cultivate a positive mental attitude and develop a smoothly functioning mind that can live in harmony with itself and the world, you must conquer fear and anxiety.

If the same fears and anxieties recur in your mind constantly and are paralyzing your efforts, seek the help of a good professional counselor. You aren't admitting weakness by doing this; you are expressing maturity and commitment to your health and your definite major purpose. A brief period of therapy may mean years of happiness.

Remember that whatever your mind can conceive and believe, it can achieve. Isn't the person who is afraid of falling on the ice the one who falls? Repeating a fear over and over in your mind makes you more susceptible to the things you fear. You must vanquish fear before it vanquishes you.

The Force of a Positive Mental Attitude

The best way to remove fear from your mind is to replace it with PMA.

Émile Coué, the French psychologist, gave us a very simple but practical formula for building PMA and maintaining a health consciousness: "Every day, in every way, I am getting better and better." Repeat this sentence to yourself many times a day until your subconscious picks it up, accepts it, and begins to carry it out in the form of good health.

This is a simple yet astounding form of autosuggestion. It depends on your belief in the statement, but the best way to build that belief is to make the statement a part of your mental environment. Remember that your mind is strongly influenced by its environment, and by filling that environment with the right thoughts, you will come to believe them.

Eating Habits

The purpose of food is to supply the body with the things it needs to maintain itself in good repair. Your eating habits must be guided by this goal alone.

Think of your digestive system as a factory. To function efficiently, it has to have a supply of a variety of materials in varying quantities. If you provide the wrong mix of materials, some jobs will never be completed, some will be done with jerry-rigged parts, and some materials will simply be stored up in every corner until the walls of the factory begin to swell. Finally the walls burst, the roof caves in, and the factory is either out of business or in need of serious and expensive repair.

Information about nutritional requirements continues to evolve as scientists work to understand more and more about the body. Pay attention to new information (but do not be swept along by fads) as it becomes available. In the main, however, some simple points will keep your diet balanced:

1. Fresh fruits and vegetables should make up the largest portion of your meals. They supply complex mixes of vitamins and trace elements, and your body is designed to avail itself of them easily.

2. Complex carbohydrates, such as breads, grains, and potatoes, should be the next largest.

3. Protein, in the form of lean meats, fish, and dairy products, is important, but it should not be the center of your meals. Select small amounts of foods you enjoy, rather than gorge yourself on steak at every meal.

4. Avoid fats; limit your intake of butter and oils, and stay away from deep-fried foods. Also avoid sugars, like candy and colas, which provide little but calories.

Seek variety as well. Your body's nutritional needs run a wide gamut, and the best way to serve those needs without becoming a food chemist is to be sure that you eat a wide spectrum of foods. Don't say, "I can't eat that way," for all you are really saying is "I don't want to eat that way." It is a very glib bit of mental gymnastics to make yourself believe that it is impossible to do what is really only unappealing or different. Why should all your efforts for success stumble over your ill health because you don't like broccoli?

Never eat while angry, frightened, or worried. Your body is simply not in a position to make use of the food when it is on a defensive footing. Worse, you can make eating a habitual response to stress, which can lead to overweight.

Moderation in food and alcohol intake is important, both because your body can be overwhelmed by an excess of either and because overindulgence can become a trick to avoid dealing with some problem that urgently needs to be faced. If you find that you cannot control either, seek the help of professionals or a worthy organization like Alcoholics or Overeaters Anonymous.

Rhythms in Relaxation

Relaxation entails completely forgetting the worries and problems of the day. As desirable as this may seem, many people have trouble relaxing.

Your conscious mind selects objects on which to concentrate, and this concentration means the exclusion of other thoughts. You cannot just collapse into a chair and announce, "I am relaxing," because your mind will select some object of focus, most often the very item you wish to forget about for a time. You need to select an object of relaxation for your mind to concentrate on. It can be kite flying, gardening, reading a novel, or anything else which will absorb you.

Television and the corner bar are not the answers. Cultivate a variety of interests that take your mind to new places. Practicing controlled meditation will do wonders for your mental powers. Physical activity can be a terrific thing to immerse yourself in; not only do you relax your mind, but you strengthen your body.

Short periods of relaxation throughout the day can break tension and give your subconscious a chance to work. Read a magazine article; listen to a language tape; work on a crossword puzzle. This is not wasting time; it is keeping your mind in top condition through relaxation.

Sleep

Your body needs time to rebuild and revitalize itself for the next day. It is sheer stupidity to try to increase your productivity by cutting your sleeping time. Six to eight hours a night are all you need. And remember that even while you sleep, your subconscious is working.

Insomnia is often caused by a failure to relax before going to bed. Don't work until you drop. Instead wind down at the end of the day by doing something you enjoy that doesn't overstimulate you. (For this reason, exercise is not good just before you go to bed.) Perhaps quiet small talk with your spouse is all you need, or an easy routine of brushing your teeth, stretching for a few moments, or making your bed. A habit which signals your body that it is time for sleep is a valuable aid.

Exercise

Ideally your relaxation and play will include exercise. Relaxing and playing are important to your mind, while exercise, which is mostly beneficial to your body, can also be of great mental benefit.

You need to engage in aerobic exercise for a period of twenty minutes at least three times a week to keep your heart and lungs strong. The rate at which you exercise must be determined by your age and physical condition; trainers at any local gym or YMCA can explain this to you and help you design a simple exercise regimen that is neither expensive nor time-consuming. (How much time do you spend watching TV?) Consult your doctor before you begin any exercise program.

Exercise can be a tremendous mental and physical stimulant, clearing away sluggishness. It also teaches you persistence and concentration. Athletic training has become an important field for understanding human potential and has resulted in many techniques that can be applied to your quest for success.

Bill Bowerman was a first-class track coach at the University of Oregon for many years; when he conceived an idea for a better running shoe, the lessons he had learned in training himself and others were an important part of making Nike the number one American shoe manufacturer.

Sex and Sublimation

Sex is your most precious and constructive drive; it is also the most easily debased. Sex is behind all the creative forces that advance human destiny. Sex has built cathedrals, universities, and nations. Why? Because the desire for sex causes us to work to please others, and out of that work spring kindness and the understanding of others.

Sex is a completely natural desire. Do not fear or deny it. But realize that you must direct it, like all desires, to definite ends instead of letting it become an end in itself. If sex is all you want, you will do anything to get it, forgetting your faith in yourself, your definite purpose, and your moral standards.

When you want sex, remember that you cannot get something for nothing. The intimacy of sex is gained by constructive work at building a committed relationship. If you channel your desire for sex into creating and providing for that relationship, you will not only get what your heart desires but also attain the heights of achievement.

To work to your greatest good, sex and sublimation need to be alternated in a rhythmical pattern, just as work and play do.

Effective Mind-Body Stimulants

At any given time your mind-body may need a boost. Many of the best boosters are things you are already doing; you just need to be conscious of the effect they have and seek them out.

• Sexual expression or a sublimated sexual drive keys up the mind so that it works rapidly and well, with real inspiration.

• Love, the ultimate aim of sexual desire, serves a similar purpose; when the two are combined, they are unbeatable.

• Fanning your burning obsession is a strong stimulant.

• Work is a wonderful opportunity for creative expression. Do something small and definite, yet satisfying, like making a phone call or writing a thank-you note.

• A burst of exercise releases pent-up energy, drives away frustration, and stimulates the brain with increased blood and oxygen.

• A little play lets the subconscious go to work.

• Music is full of rhythms, beats, and pulses. You can select it to boost your enthusiasm or help you calm down.

• Friendship is a great stimulant. Talk your problems over with others. Laugh with them.

• Your children can inspire you. Build a strong relationship with them, and never neglect to spend as much time with them as possible. Teach your children a skill, and renew your self-confidence. Let your children talk to you, and renew your faith.

• Mastermind alliances are powerful stimulants. Seek out the enthusiasm and experience of other people when you need a boost. Mutual suffering causes people to pool their mind power and direct it to relieve that suffering.

• Autosuggestion implants the ideas you want in your mind. Use it whenever you need it.

• Faith and religion are stimulants of the noblest order. Turn to the assurances they offer you and renew your sense of purpose.

Your mental and physical health is inseparable. You cannot work to strengthen one without having a positive effect on the other. Your mind and your body are the navigator and the ship which carry you to the success you desire. Do everything you can to preserve, protect, and defend them.

✦ 16 ✦

BUDGET YOUR TIME
AND MONEY

A Personal Inventory
✦
Doers and Drifters
✦
How a Doer Uses Time
✦
Some Doers You Should Know
✦
The Division of Your Day
✦
Time Management on the Job
✦
Budgeting Your Spare Time
✦
Budgeting Your Money

Tell me how you use your time and how you spend your money, and I will tell you where and what you will be ten years from now.

Time and money are precious resources, and few people striving for success ever believe they possess either one in excess. Understanding how you use them is an important part of evaluating your progress toward success and analyzing what may be holding you back.

We'll begin this chapter by taking an inventory of your

progress toward success with a special emphasis on the role of time. Once you've seen how to improve your use of time, you'll be able to devote more of it to managing your money. And any review of the overall path you are following is always valuable.

A Personal Inventory

Ask the following questions of yourself, and answer them honestly; you want to identify areas needing improvement, not win a prize for a high ranking. Feeding your ego by lying to yourself about the truth will only waste the time you spend on the inventory and undermine your self-confidence.

1. Do you have a major definite purpose? What plans do you have for attaining it? How much time are you devoting to those plans on a persistent, daily basis? How often do you work on your plans; only when the notion strikes you or when you can snatch a few minutes during commercials?

2. Is your definite major purpose a burning obsession? When and how often do you fan its flames?

3. What have you planned to give in return for realizing your definite major purpose? Are you doing it yet? When will you start?

4. What steps have you taken to build your mastermind alliance? How often are you in contact with the members? How many of them do you speak to monthly, weekly, and daily?

5. Have you made a habit of accepting temporary defeat as a challenge to greater effort? (Let's hope your temporary defeats are few, but they are inevitable.) How quickly do you seek out the seed of equivalent benefit when adversity strikes?

6. How do you spend more of your time: carrying out your plans or brooding over the obstacles you face?

7. How often do you forgo personal pleasure in order to have more time to work on your plan? How often is it the other way around?

8. Do you seize every moment of time as if it were the only one you were sure you had?

9. Have you looked at your life as the result of the way you spent time in the past? Are you happy with your life to date? Do you wish you had spent it some other way? Do you regard each second that passes as the opportunity to change the course of your life for the better?

10. Is your mental attitude always positive? Is it positive most of the time? Some of the time? Is it positive now? Can you make it positive in the next second? How about the one after that?

11. How often do you display personal initiative by backing your positive thoughts with action?

12. Do you believe that you will succeed by luck or a windfall? When are these things going to happen? Do you believe that you will succeed as the result of your own efforts? When are you going to make those efforts?

13. Do you know anyone who inspires you with his or her personal initiative? How often do you seek that person out? How often do you actually model your behavior on him or her?

14. When do you go the extra mile? Does it happen every day or just when you think someone is paying attention? Is your attitude good when you do it, or do you begrudge the additional work?

15. How attractive is your personality? Do you look at yourself in the mirror every morning and work to improve your smile, your facial expressions? Or do you just brush up before an important meeting?

16. How are you applying your faith? When do you act on the inspiration from Infinite Intelligence? How often do you ignore it?

17. Are you building your self-discipline? How often do

uncontrolled emotions cause you to do something you quickly regret?

18. Have you mastered your fears? How often do you display their symptoms? When do you replace them with your ambitions?

19. How often do you accept other people's opinions as fact? Do you question those opinions every time you encounter them? How often do you call on accurate thinking as the solution to your problems?

20. How often do you inspire cooperation by giving it? Are you doing it at home? At the office? In your mastermind alliance?

21. What opportunities do you allow your imagination? When do you apply yourself to problems with creative vision? What dilemmas do you have that need to be solved this way?

22. Are you relaxing, exercising, and paying attention to your health? Were you planning to start at the new year? Why can't you start right now?

This inventory is designed to get you thinking. Your use of your time reflects the degree to which you have made the principles of personal achievement a part of your life. Don't be discouraged if your answers to these questions are not yet what you'd like them to be. I have sold books to millions of people and lectured to thousands more. Many of them gained great success afterward, but none of them did it overnight. Although the benefits from success can accrue very quickly, most truly successful people need much of a lifetime to get everything they want. Those are lifetimes well spent.

Doers and Drifters

Your attitude toward life determines your attitude toward time. People pretty much fall into two camps on this subject.

Doers:

- Have a definite major purpose
- Manage circumstances and resources
- Examine every idea they encounter before they adopt or discard it
- Take risks and assume responsibility
- Learn from their mistakes
- Go the extra mile
- Control their habits
- Have positive mental attitudes
- Apply their faith in their own success
- Create mastermind alliances to expand their knowledge and experience
- Recognize their weaknesses and take steps to correct them

Drifters:

- Have no goal in life
- Are controlled by circumstances and the lack of resources
- Flit from one idea about life to the other, depending on this week's fad or what the guy on TV said last night
- Run from opportunity and blame others for their lots in life
- Make the same mistakes again and again
- Do only what it takes to get by
- Let their habits control them
- Have negative mental attitudes
- Never do anything to improve their situation
- Learn all they want to know from that guy on TV
- Wouldn't know a weakness if it bit them

How a Doer Uses Time

My guess is that if you've made it this far, you're determined to be a doer. Great! Let's look at some places where a
doer can make substantial difference in his or her life by the
wise use of time.

Occupation

A doer sees work as the source of all opportunity, a route
to independence and security, and a means to better the surrounding world. Doers select work suited to their education
and temperaments; they engage in labors of love.

Doers don't evaluate their work by the number of hours it
takes. They look at it from the perspective of the amount of
useful service they render by going the extra mile. Time is a
tool for them, not an end. They take pride in their achievements, not in bursting out the door at 4:59:59. They don't
complain about long hours; they complain that the hours
aren't long enough to accomplish everything they want.

As a result, doers get paid twice. Not only do they take
checks home, but they also earn the right to better jobs and
bigger checks.

Mental Habits

Doers take possession of their minds through self-
discipline. They make plans, and they carry them out. They
direct their minds toward the objects of their desire, and they
keep their minds occupied with those things. They don't
spend time thinking about what they don't want.

Doers recharge their positive mental attitudes often. Their
productivity gives them concrete signs of their progress toward their goals. They take these signs as indications of the
great things just over the horizon.

Relationships

A doer inspires cooperation from others by giving it first. Doers don't spend time arguing, nitpicking, or gossiping. And they avoid people who do.

Doers don't waste their time with drifters. They realize that defeatist attitudes can be contagious, and they don't want to be infected. They aren't selfish; they're just *particular*.

Instead they associate with people who are willing to work with them. They offer those people the extra-mile service they offer everyone. In return they gain enthusiasm and support.

Doers have sympathy for drifters. They'll even point the way toward definiteness or purpose and lend a hand to anyone who has gained just that much. But they know that they can't help someone who isn't ready to help himself or herself.

They also delegate work. Doers know that you should never do anything which you can get someone else to do for you better than you can do it. They realize they have to be available to the people who are working with them, and they offer those people all the access they need.

Health

Doers pay attention to their mental and physical health. They relax, they exercise, they eat right, and they see the doctor when something goes wrong.

The doer knows that time spent in prevention is much shorter than time spent on repair. Doers don't begrudge themselves the benefits of sound minds and bodies.

Religion

Doers are people of active faith. They let their commitment to leading their lives morally and honorably insulate them from fear and arrogance. Their consciences don't have reason to reproach them because they spend all their time in constructive efforts.

In addition, doers are people of every religion. No matter what their convictions are, they live by them to the fullest extent. Whenever they face problems, they turn to those convictions and make their decisions based upon them. They are not paralyzed by doubt, and they can act immediately.

Spare Time

Doers put the time they have away from their jobs to practical uses. They romance their spouses, laugh with their children, relax alone, exercise with friends, educate themselves, campaign for good political candidates, or work on their plans for their definite major purposes.

The doer is not a workaholic. Doers know that there are other things in life besides their own immediate success. They know that if they don't pay attention to those things, their success will be meaningless.

But doers don't engage in activities that have no payoffs. They aren't likely to be found in front of the television sets for four hours a night. There aren't many doers who have their own barstools either.

Doers enjoy life more than drifters do because everything they do brings them closer to their goals. They make all their time work for them. Doers see movies, read books, go to basketball games, even stare up into the blue sky and watch the clouds go by. *But they know why they are doing it.* That makes all the difference between a doer and a drifter, and it's all the difference between a success and a failure.

Some Doers You Should Know

William Sydney Porter sat in his prison cell contemplating the stupidity of the embezzlement that had brought him there. As near as he could figure, the only thing he had gained was a lot of spare time. And since he had several years left in his term, there didn't seem to be a lot he could do with it.

But there was, and Porter did it. He began to write short stories. He wrote many of them. Then he began to sell those short stories to magazines under the name O. Henry. By the time he was released, he was already the most popular short story writer in the country. He walked out of prison into a success.

Warren Avis was a doer. As an air force officer, he was constantly travelling the country and he recognized how convenient it would be for people to be able to rent a car right at the airport. While his $10,000 in savings wasn't enough money to set up an operation on his own, he did have the gumption to put together a business plan and get a bank loan. Within eight years he had car-rental counters in airports across America and was able to sell the company for almost eight million dollars. Avis saw an 800 percent return on his investment because he was willing to do all the work necessary to make that chance pay off.

One of these men started off serving a jail term, the other serving his country. But they both recognized that in order to make their lives amount to something, they had to become doers by taking control of their time.

The Division of Your Day

We each get twenty-four hours to manage. The broad divisions of that time are easy to see:

1. Eight hours for sleep
2. Eight hours for work
3. Eight hours of spare time

You can't mess around much with the first division or your health will suffer. You can occasionally steal an hour or two from your sleep, but it's a bad habit. Don't create any bad habits.

The eight hours spent at work are potentially your most directly productive. You need to stay focused on your purpose and your habit of going the extra mile if this is to be the case. The preceding fifteen chapters of this book will teach you that. But in a few lines I'll give you some tips to manage that time more effectively in attaining your purpose.

The last eight hours are your spare time. You need to manage them as well, or you'll find them slipping away in routine household chores, reruns of *Mr. Ed,* and listening to your neighbor talk about his new lawn mower again. This can be harder, but I have some guidelines to offer.

As you'll see, managing your time—like managing your life—requires knowing what you want to use it for.

Time Management on the Job

As our society gets more complicated, there seems to be more to do. I am indebted to the writings of Alan Lakein and Stephanie Winston for some of the advice that follows; they've spent their time learning about time.

Prioritizing Your Tasks

Make a list of all the things you need to do today, this week, and this month. Divide another sheet of paper into four equal sections. Label the top left "Important and Urgent." Here you will enter jobs that you know must be done right away in order for you to be successful. Write the day and hour each task is due next to each job.

Label the top right section "Important but Not Urgent." Put things here that are essential to your work but aren't a crisis. If you pay the most attention to this section, nothing should end up in the top left category. Again, make a note next to each task about just exactly when it has to be done. *It is important to review this section every day so that nothing slips over into "Important and Urgent."*

In the bottom left, write "Unimportant but Urgent." This category, like the last one, requires you to have a keen sense of your purpose. You have to be able to make a definite decision about what matters to you. Most of things that fall into it will be spontaneous: Someone will want your advice; you may get a call telling you that you have to *act now* to buy that beautiful time share in the Poconos. You won't bother to write them down because you can either dismiss them or move them into "Important and Urgent." The category is on the sheet of paper mostly to remind you that "urgent" does not mean "important."

Finally write "Unimportant and Not Urgent" in the bottom right. You might not even bother to write tasks down here since it means that you will never devote attention to them. But again, it helps to remind yourself that there are many things which can fall into this category.

When you complete a task, put a line through it. Create evidence of your accomplishment as a reminder of your efficient use of your time.

Handling Paper

Two kinds of paper will cross your desk: valuable (a sales update) and superfluous (information about the office pool). Throw the superfluous stuff away without even setting it back down on your desk. Never give it a second thought.

Handle the valuable material as little as possible. If you can, attend to it right then and there. Read updates, sign authorizations, write responses on the spot. Put reading material like magazine articles aside for a regular, dedicated time.

If you can't act on a paper for some reason, make a small dot in an upper corner. The next time you pick it up, make another dot. You'll soon see how often you're handling the same piece of paper again, and you'll be motivated to do something about it.

Budgeting Your Spare Time

Routine tasks will easily expand to fit the time available and eat up all your spare time unless you make a definite decision to devote it to the things you think are important.

Allot your time in the following manner to make sure that you are able to do all the things you need to:

1. Spend one hour a day in quiet meditation on the following subjects.
a. Your plan for your definite major purpose
b. Contact with Infinite Intelligence, affirming your gratitude for the blessings you have
c. Self-analysis; identifying the fears you need to master and making plans for doing so
d. Ways to increase harmony in all your relationships
e. The things you desire instead of the things you don't want
2. Devote two hours to going the extra mile by rendering some sort of service to your community, your spouse, or your family without expecting any kind of reward for it.
3. Study and read for self-improvement for an hour.
4. Spend an hour in contact with members of your mastermind alliance or close personal friends.

This leaves three hours for relaxation, recreation, exercise, and other responsibilities.

As you become familiar with these activities, you may be able to combine them with other things. You can meditate or read while commuting on the bus or train; if you have to drive to work, listen to audiotapes of self-improvement books. Carpool with a member of your mastermind alliance, and use the driving time for discussion and problem solving.

If your relaxation involves a worthwhile hobby, teach it to youngsters in local service groups, rendering extra service to your community. The possibilities are as many as you can make them.

Follow this schedule six days a week, and set aside one day for nothing but mental and physical relaxation and your religious and philosophical activities. You can spend much of this time with your family. You all will be glad you did.

Budgeting Your Money

Many people have written good and valuable books about specific ways of managing your money. Seek them out. I won't provide you with the nitty-gritty details, but I will remind you of the importance of budgeting your money.

Like time, money should be spent with a definite purpose in mind. You must create a budget for all your expenses, and you must use self-discipline in sticking to it.

Your first priority in any budget should be to set aside a fixed percentage of your income for savings. The rule is "Pay yourself first." A strong and growing savings cushion is an important weapon in your fight against the fear of poverty. If adversity or ill health strikes, adequate savings will allow you to start looking for the seed of equivalent benefit right away. You won't panic about the mortgage payment, and you'll be able to recover more quickly.

Make sure that you have adequate life insurance if others depend on you. The cost of a good policy is worth the anguish you will save your dependents. Your sudden departure from this life will be more than enough sadness for them; don't compound it with the threat of the poorhouse.

Allocate some portion of your income to charity. This is an important part of going the extra mile. Let's hope you never have to depend on some worthy group to help you out, but what right do you have to anyone's aid if you have never given any help yourself?

If you're in debt, you need to spend as much as you can realistically afford to pay that debt off. Don't tell yourself that you'll need only ten dollars a week spending money when you've been blowing a hundred, because once you spend that eleventh dollar, you'll decide you've already blown your budget and might as well go all the way. It's a slippery slope. And don't cut into your savings allotment to pay your debts either. Make savings a habit. Never back away from a good habit.

Once you're out of debt, divide the money you were using to pay it off between your savings and your general household and entertainment expenses. You want to cultivate the habit of increasing your savings whenever your income rises, but you should also give yourself some immediate reward for doing your job.

You will probably find that circumstances arise that your budget did not allow for. There may be a health emergency, a new baby on the way, a parent who needs help. Don't let this throw you. By developing and sticking to your budget, you've increased your habit of self-discipline. You've also learned to make your money serve your purpose. You did it before, and you can do it again.

Habits are an important part of budgeting your time and money. They're important to every principle in the science of personal achievement; they are, in fact, the keys to all personal achievement. The next chapter will teach you to select and control your habits on the basis of cosmic law.

✦ 17 ✦

USE COSMIC
HABITFORCE

Using Natural Forces

✦

Moneymaking Habits

✦

Flexible Habits

✦

Beware of These Habits

✦

Embrace These Habits

✦

Controlling Your Willpower

✦

The Three Essentials of Cosmic Habitforce

You are where you are and what you are because of your established habits.

The aim of this book has been to force you to examine those habits and to teach you ways to change them. To do this, you need to understand and apply a universal principle I call cosmic habitforce.

Cosmic habitforce is the law which makes every living creature, every particle of matter subject to the influence of its environment. It can work for you or against you. The choice is yours.

Using Natural Forces

The grandest example of cosmic habitforce is the operation of the heavens. Stars and planets move with clocklike precision. They don't collide; they don't suddenly veer off course (at least, not without some major change in the forces at work, like a supernova or a black hole, which are themselves just another example of matter behaving according to established patterns). A complex system of gravity and inertia, attraction and repulsion keeps things moving so precisely that for millennia human beings have been able to predict the position of the stars and planets, the timing of eclipses, and the regularity of meteor showers.

Sunflowers don't grow from turnip seeds; giraffes don't give birth to tadpoles; clouds don't release milk. Everything does that which is its nature to do.

All this is a reflection of universal order, which makes so much of the physical operation of the world understandable. Certainly we are still working to understand more than we already do, but science is based on the faith that there is universal order. All actions and reactions are fixed on the basis of this order.

In the science of personal achievement you seek to take control of this order by taking control of your habits. You recognize that your thoughts and actions will become as much a part of your nature as Pluto's orbit is a part of its nature. If your habits are positive, the seeds that they plant will be, too.

But you have to realize that cosmic habitforce always operates. If your habits are negative, their results will also be negative. This is why you must take control of your habits through self-discipline.

Habits become a part of your nature by repetition. If you create thought habits by repeating certain ideas in your mind, cosmic habitforce will take over those patterns of thought, make them more or less permanent (depending on your intensity of repetition and practice), and put them to work. The same thing will happen with physical habits.

If you follow the same route to and from work every day, you make that route a habit. You probably aren't even aware that it is a habit until you need to alter your route to go to a store or visit a friend. If you aren't paying attention when you start your trip, you will probably find yourself missing the turn or forgetting your task altogether. This is an example of why you need to be aware of and in control of all your habits.

If your dominating mental habits are thoughts of poverty, then cosmic habitforce will bring about poverty in your life. If your dominating mental habits are of prosperity and peace, cosmic habitforce will bring them about.

There is an endless cycle here. Repetition of a habit intensifies it until it becomes an obsession. You can become obsessed with poverty or with achievement. This is why I have repeatedly stressed that *your thoughts are the only thing you can completely control if you decide to do so*. You must control your thoughts to control your habits.

Cosmic habitforce doesn't leave you any room to complain that opportunity never came your way. You will know that as long as you have the power to form and express your thoughts, you have the power to change the circumstances of your life into whatever you want them to be.

If your life isn't already what you want it to be, it is because you have drifted into your present circumstances by virtue of cosmic habitforce. You can change that. Definiteness of purpose, backed by the power of cosmic habitforce and enforced by self-discipline and personal initiative, can bring you to the circumstances you want.

Moneymaking Habits

So the circumstances you want include making more money, do they? Here's how to go about using cosmic habitforce to do just that.

Step one. Create a clear mental image of just how much money you want to make. "A lot" is not a good answer. You need a concrete figure or a percentage above your current income.

Step two. Imagine some of the results of having that money: a new home, sending your daughter to medical school, a comfortable retirement. Doing this clarifies which of the ten basic motives are driving you (see page 18 for the list). The more motives you can associate with making more money, the stronger your push to achieve it.

Step three. Decide how you will earn this extra money. I've emphasized again and again that you can't get something for nothing. You must have a plan.

Step four. Write out your goal and your plan. Include your motives for making more money. Instead of a statement like "I want to retire in security," write something like "I want to own my home free and clear of debt; I want to be able to travel and visit my family three times a year." Set a date for starting and achieving this goal. Sign your plan; make it a contract with yourself.

Step five. Go back to your plan, and underline all the things that you need to do to make it happen that you aren't doing now. Make a separate list of these things.

Step six. Start doing the things on this list. Some of them will be daily tasks, such as spending less money on dining out and putting more money into your savings account. Others will be longer-range but will require daily progress, such as going the extra mile in your job. You have to bend all your efforts and thoughts to doing these things.

Step seven. Every day read your goal aloud to yourself until you have it memorized. Repeat it in your mind when you get out of bed, when you start your job, when you come back from lunch, when your workday is finished, and before you go to sleep.

Yes, this is just what you should be doing anyway in connection with your definite major purpose. You are giving cosmic habitforce a pattern to follow. The length of time you need to start conditioning your mind to get positive results depends almost entirely on the amount of faith and enthusiasm you place behind your words and actions. All voluntary positive habits are the products of willpower directed toward the attainment of definite goals.

If you say to yourself, "Sometime in my life I want a hundred thousand dollars," you are saying, "I am uncertain about my goals." Here cosmic habitforce cannot come into play because there is no definite pattern for it to follow. If you say instead, "Six months from now I want a hundred thousand dollars, and I will do X, Y, and Z to get it," cosmic habitforce has a pattern to follow. But it will follow that pattern only when your thoughts and actions lead it there. If you don't do X, Y, and Z, you won't develop cosmic habitforce.

Flexible Habits

Be sure to make your plan sufficiently flexible so that you can change it when you are so inspired. The key word here is "inspired." As you put your plan into action and develop applied faith, Infinite Intelligence may hand you a better plan than the one you have made. Treat such inspiration respectfully, for it will help you strengthen your plan where it is weak.

Don't express contempt for your hunches. If you repeatedly say to yourself, "I had the most foolish idea today," soon you will be having only foolish ideas. Instead write down your hunches as soon as they occur to you. Examine them carefully, and be sure you are not rejecting them simply because they involve something that hasn't been done before or because they don't conform to your current habits.

The purpose of cosmic habitforce is to make your habits serve you, not the other way around. Don't let your habits become so ingrained that whatever useful purpose they once served, they now limit your opportunity, tolerance, faith, and enthusiasm.

American Express enjoyed huge success with its charge card in the 1980s. It became a symbol of prestige, and millions of new members signed on. More businesses than ever accepted the card because they wanted to attract card members' dollars. Then the economy changed, but American Express's habits didn't.

As it became necessary to stretch every penny and to watch every percentage of margin, cardholders began switching from the high-fee American Express card to no-fee cards from Visa and MasterCard that offered almost the same benefits. Merchants became angry because American Express claimed a higher percentage of each charge than other cards; worse, it was slow to credit merchants' accounts.

The number of cardholders began to fall dramatically. In Boston a group of restaurants even organized a boycott of American Express to protest its policies toward merchants. Profits disappeared, and losses mounted.

Cosmic habitforce was at work. American Express kept doing business the way it always had until a crisis hit it right between the eyes. The habits that had made it the premier charge card were not the habits that would *keep* it the premier charge card. Its habits ruled them, not the other way around.

Whatever your habits, cosmic habitforce will carry them out. It isn't enough merely to develop good habits and leave it at that. You must remain alert to the effect of your habits and be willing on a moment's notice to change them when new ones will serve you better.

Beware of These Habits

The good news is, ironically, if you have any of these habits, they will eventually cause some sort of defeat that will inspire you to eliminate them. Of course, you can spare yourself that trouble if you're willing to examine yourself, identify your negative habits, and resolve to replace them with positive ones.

- Poverty
- Imaginary illness
- Laziness
- Envy
- Greed
- Vanity
- Cynicism
- Drifting without aim or purpose
- Irritability
- Revenge
- Jealousy
- Dishonesty
- Arrogance
- Sadism

Embrace These Habits

You can replace any of the above with one of the following and profit by doing it.

- Definiteness of purpose. This is the primary good habit. It makes you more alert, more imaginative, more enthusiastic, and it increases your willpower.
- Faith. Let your mind dwell on positive ideas and on clearing away all negative influences and fears. This takes self-discipline.

• Personal initiative. You may have to force yourself at first to do things without being told to do them. But persistence will make it easier.

• Enthusiasm. Remember that *controlled* enthusiasm is your goal. You'll want to be able to summon it at will or shut it off when it isn't appropriate or might actually be dangerous.

• Self-discipline. This is a circular process; the more you exercise it, the more you have it.

• Going the extra mile. Start right now by doing something for which you don't expect to be paid directly. Go the extra mile every day by sheer effort if necessary, and soon the effort will be replaced by habit.

Controlling Your Willpower

In the chapter on self-discipline you learned about your ego, the source of your willpower. Developing positive habits which can be taken over by cosmic habitforce depends heavily on strong willpower. Here's a review of the steps to strengthen your will:

Step one. Actively ally yourself with other people who can help you attain your major purpose. A mastermind alliance creates multiple patterns for cosmic habitforce to work on.

Step two. Develop your plan, drawing on all the members of your alliance for knowledge, ability, and the power of their faith.

Step three. Distance yourself from anyone and any circumstance that make you feel inferior. A positive ego does not grow in a negative environment. Remember that cosmic habitforce causes every living thing to partake of the dominating influence of its environment.

Step four. Close the door on the unpleasant experiences of the past. A strong will doesn't dwell on the past; a vital ego thrives on hopes and desires of an as-yet-unattained objective. If you keep your mind in a state of hope and desire, cosmic habitforce goes to work changing your hopes and desires into their material equivalent.

Step five. Surround yourself with every possible means of impressing your mind with the nature of your definite purpose. Hang mottoes on your walls; put up pictures of people doing what you want to do. You want to make it easier to create a mental image of yourself realizing your objective. The more you create this image, the sooner it will be taken over by cosmic habitforce and impressed on your subconscious.

Step six. Watch out that you don't overinflate your ego. One small prick with a pin and the escaping hot air will be like a runaway rocket, carrying you far away from where you want to be.

The Three Essentials of Cosmic Habitforce

Three qualities underlie the process of voluntary establishment of a habit.

Plasticity

This is the capability to change. It also implies that once a change has been made, your new form will hold until a subsequent change is made; you won't revert to your old status. Consider the difference between modeling clay, which is malleable but holds the shape it is given, and mercury, which can take any shape for a moment but will never keep it.

You can be changed by environmental influences or by your own decisions.

Frequency of Impression

Repetition is the mother of habit. One of the factors affecting the speed with which a habit can be adopted is how often it is consciously repeated. Your ability to do this may vary with circumstances. Your job may require enough concentration on the task at hand that you have to pay attention only to it and develop your habits in your spare time. Personal initiative also comes into play; if you're lazy, you won't knock yourself out developing a habit. This can definitely slow down the process of acquiring it.

Intensity of Impression

You can go through the motions of an activity, or you can concentrate on doing it; concentration builds the habit quickly. You impress the habit on your subconscious mind, and it becomes a part of everything you do.

Here's an example of these three essentials at work. A woman working the swing shift at an electronics assembly plant was allowed two ten-minute breaks, one at 6:00 P.M. and one at 10:30. Most of her coworkers used these breaks for cigarettes. She didn't want to cultivate a bad habit that would affect her health and make her a less pleasing personality, so she decided instead to have a snack. Her garden was in full bloom, so she would have a carrot, an apple, or something else she had grown herself.

Being human, she already had plasticity; it's part of everyone's nature. Every day, throughout the summer and fall, precisely at 6:00 and at 10:30, she would have her snack. This gave a definite frequency of impression.

The element of intensity varied according to her relative hunger. Sometimes she ate with relish because her meal at home had been small. Sometimes she skipped a meal before coming to work, and the intensity of her hunger was even greater. But whenever the break came, she ate, no matter how hungry she was.

As the months passed, she realized that regardless of what she had eaten, she got hungry before her breaks. She watched the clock, waiting for a chance to eat. Sometimes it seemed the time would never come. And when her garden was no longer producing good, fresh food, she switched to anything else she had at home: a candy bar, a doughnut, cookies.

This is a clear example of the voluntary establishment of a habit. But it wasn't really a good habit. She began to put on weight and found she was distracted from her work for half an hour before her breaks.

So she decided to break her habit and stopped bringing food. This wasn't the answer because there was food in the vending machines at the plant, and she just started buying that. Not only was she still eating, but she was now spending more money to do it.

At this point she really had to seize possession of her mind, inspire it with a strong motive, and take definite action. She set a definite minor purpose to break her habit. She did this by reading, substituting the desire for knowledge and inspiration for the desire for food. When her break came, she reached for a book instead of a candy bar. The same frequency of impression was there, of course. The only thing different was the intensity. At first the feeling of hunger persisted, but after a few days she acquired an appetite for reading which overwhelmed the old physical desire. She established a new habit to supplant the old.

Any worthless, superfluous, or harmful habit can be broken and replaced with a more desirable one if you want it to be so. The nucleus of the entire science of personal achievement lies in this concept. Cosmic habitforce is the means for incorporating every one of the Seventeen Principles of Success into your life. Control your mental attitude, keep it positive by exercising self-discipline, and prepare your mental soil so that any worthwhile plan, purpose, or desire may be planted by repeated, intense impression. Know that it will germinate, grow, and find expression, bringing you whatever it is you want from life.

**WHATEVER YOUR MIND CAN CONCEIVE AND BELIEVE,
YOUR MIND CAN ACHIEVE.**

◆ 18 ◆

THE SEVENTEEN PRINCIPLES OF SUCCESS

A Fast Review

The list that follows is meant to serve as a reminder. Look it over once a week. Are you making regular progress in each of these areas? If you routinely evaluate your efforts to embrace the principles, you are less likely to be caught in a crisis because you've neglected to think accurately, for instance, or to find that your coworkers suddenly regard you as an opportunistic shark.

1. Develop definiteness of purpose.
2. Establish a mastermind alliance.
3. Assemble an attractive personality.
4. Use applied faith.
5. Go the extra mile.
6. Create personal initiative.
7. Build a positive mental attitude.
8. Control your enthusiasm.

9. Enforce self-discipline.
10. Think accurately.
11. Control your attention.
12. Inspire teamwork.
13. Learn from adversity and defeat.
14. Cultivate creative vision.
15. Maintain sound health.
16. Budget your time and money.
17. Use cosmic habitforce.

A Detailed Evaluation

Following are concise summaries of the steps to making each principle a part of your life. Read them through and then use the lines provided at the end of each section to write down specific actions you plan to take to implement the principles.

The summaries themselves will give you concrete recommendations about what to do. Under the definiteness of purpose you might write down that you will define your major goal, write out a plan for achieving it, and read that plan aloud to yourself every day, all of which are mentioned in the summary. But if you also include a date by which you will have your plan written down, you will be making a commitment to yourself that will provide you with extra motivation. So do not simply parrot back the summary's suggestions; consider carefully the changes you need to make and be as detailed as possible in writing them out. In a few weeks or months you can look at these notes, recognize the progress you've made, and renew your commitment to success.

1. Develop DEFINITENESS OF PURPOSE— with PMA

The Starting Point of All Worthwhile Achievements

You should have one high, desirable, outstanding goal, and keep it ever before you. You can have many nonconflicting goals which help you to reach your major definite goal. It is advisable to have immediate, intermediate, and distant objectives. When you set a definite major goal, you are apt to recognize that which will help you achieve it.

Determine or fix in your mind exactly what you desire. Be definite.

Evaluate and determine exactly what you will give in return.

Set a definite date for exactly when you intend to possess your desire.

Identify your desire with a definite plan for carrying out and achieving your objective. Put your plan into *action* at once.

Clearly define your plan for achievement. Write out precisely and concisely *exactly* what you want, *exactly* when you want to achieve it, and *exactly* what you intend to give in return.

Each and every day, morning and evening, read your written statement aloud. As you read it, see, feel, and *believe* yourself already in possession of your objective.

Engage in personal inspection with regularity to determine whether you are on the right track and headed in the right direction so that you don't deviate from the path that leads to the achievement of your objective.

To guarantee success, engage daily in study, thinking, and planning time with PMA regarding yourself and your family and how you can achieve your definite goals.

WHATEVER YOUR MIND CAN CONCEIVE AND BELIEVE, YOU CAN ACHIEVE—WHEN YOU HAVE PMA AND APPLY IT.

My commitment to use this principle in my life is:

_____

_____

_____

_____

2. Establish A Mastermind Alliance—with PMA

A mastermind alliance is two or more minds working together in the spirit of perfect harmony toward the attainment of a specific objective.

This principle makes it possible for you, through association with others, to acquire and utilize the knowledge and experience needed for the attainment of any desired goal in life.

Your mastermind alliance can be created by surrounding yourself or aligning yourself with the advice, counsel, and personal cooperation of several people who are willing to lend you their wholehearted aid for the attainment of your objective in the spirit of perfect harmony.

You can create a mastermind alliance with your spouse, your manager, a friend, a coworker, etc. Once a mastermind alliance is formed, the group as a whole must become and remain active. The group must move in a definite plan, at a definite time, toward a definite common objective. Indecision, inactivity, or delay will destroy the usefulness of the alliance. There must be a complete meeting of the minds without reservations on the part of any member.

You can have several mastermind alliances, each with different objectives—i.e., an alliance with your spouse to reach your family objectives, an alliance with your banker or investment counselor or attorney for your financial objectives, an alliance with your minister or clergy for your spiritual objectives, etc.

My commitment to use this principle in my life is:

_____

_____

_____

_____

3. Assemble an ATTRACTIVE PERSONALITY— with PMA

Your personality is your greatest asset or greatest liability, for it embraces everything that you control: mind, body, and soul. A person's personality is the person. It shapes the nature of your thoughts, your deeds, your relationships with others, and it establishes the boundaries of the space you occupy in the world.

It is essential that you develop a pleasing personality— pleasing to yourself and to others.

It is imperative that you develop the habit of being sensitive to your own reactions to individuals, circumstances, and events and to the reactions of individuals and groups to what you say, think, or do.

Positive Factors of a Pleasing Personality

A positive mental attitude
Tolerance
Alertness
Common courtesy
A fondness for people
Flexibility
Tactfulness
Personal magnetism
A pleasant tone of voice
Control of facial expressions
Sportsmanship
Sincerity
A sense of humor
Humility of the heart
Smiling
Enthusiasm
Control of temper and emotions
Patience
Proper dress

DO UNTO OTHERS AS YOU WOULD HAVE OTHERS
DO UNTO YOU.

My commitment to use this principle in my life is:

_____

_____

_____

_____

4. Use APPLIED FAITH—with PMA

Faith is a state of mind through which your aims, desires, plans, and purposes may be translated into their physical or financial equivalent.

Applied faith means *action*—specifically, the habit of applying your faith under any and all circumstances. It is faith in your God, yourself, your fellowman—and the unlimited opportunities available to you.

Faith without *action* is dead. Faith is the art of *believing by doing*. It comes as a result of persistent *action*. Fear and doubt are faith in reverse gear. Faith, in its positive application, is the key which will give one direct communications with Infinite Intelligence.

Applied faith is belief in an objective or purpose backed by unqualified activity. If you want results, try a prayer. When you pray, express your gratitude, and thanksgiving for the blessings you already have received; then ask the Good Lord for his help. Affirm the objectives of your desires through prayer each night and morning. Inspire your imagination to see yourself already in possession of them, and act precisely as if you were already in physical possession of them. The possession of anything first takes place mentally by being imagined in the mind's eye.

PRAYER IS YOUR GREATEST POWER!

My commitment to use this principle in my life is:

_____

_____

_____

_____

5. Go the EXTRA MILE—with PMA

Render more and better service for which you are paid, and do it with a positive mental attitude. Form the habit of going the extra mile because of the pleasure you get out of it and because of what it does to you and for you deep down inside. It is inevitable that every seed of useful service you sow will multiply itself and come back to you in overwhelming abundance.

Following this principle will make you indispensable to other people. The principle manifests itself in two important laws: the Law of Compensation and the Law of Increasing Returns. These unvarying laws always reward intelligent effort rendered in the attitude of faith and rendered instinctively without regards to the limits of immediate compensation.

$$Q^1 + Q^2 + MA = C$$

The quality of the service rendered plus the quantity of the service rendered plus the mental attitude in which it is rendered equals your compensation in the world and the amount of space you will occupy in the hearts of your fellow man.

MAKE GOING THE EXTRA MILE WITH PMA A HABIT!

My commitment to use this principle in my life is:

_____

_____

_____

_____

6. Create PERSONAL INITIATIVE—with PMA

Personal initiative is the inner power that starts all *action*. It is the power that inspires the completion of that which one begins. It is the dynamo that starts the faculty of the imagination into *action*.

It is, in fact, *Self-motivation*.

Motivation is that which induces *action* or determines choice. It is that which provides a motive. A motive is that inner urge only within the individual which incites you to *action*, such as an idea, an emotion, a desire, or an impulse. It is a hope or other force which starts in an attempt to produce specific results.

When you know principles that can motivate you, you will then know principles that can motivate others.

Motivate yourself with PMA. Hope is the magic ingredient in motivation, but the secret of accomplishment is getting into *action*.

USE AND DEVELOP THE SELF-STARTER. DO IT NOW!

My commitment to use this principle in my life is:

_____
_____
_____
_____

7. Build a POSITIVE MENTAL ATTITUDE

PMA stands for "positive mental attitude."

A positive mental attitude is the *right, honest, constructive thought, action,* or *reaction* to any person, situation, or set of circumstances that does not violate the laws of God or the right of one's fellowman.

PMA allows you to build on hope and overcome the negative attitudes of despair and discouragement. It gives you the mental power, the feeling, the confidence to do anything you make up your mind to do. PMA is commonly referred to as the "I can . . . I will" attitude applicable to all challenging circumstances in your life.

You create and maintain a positive mental attitude through your own willpower, based on motives of your own adaption. To develop PMA, strive to understand and apply the Golden Rule; be considerate and sensitive to the reactions of others; be sensitive to your own reactions by controlling your emotional responses; be a good finder; believe that any goal can be achieved; and develop what are understood to be right habits of thought and action.

A positive mental attitude is the catalyst necessary for achieving worthwhile success. Achievement is attained through some combination of PMA and definiteness of purpose with one or more of the other fifteen success principles.

MAINTAIN THE RIGHT ATTITUDE—A POSITIVE MENTAL ATTITUDE.

My commitment to use this principle in my life is:

_____

_____

_____

_____

8. Control Your Enthusiasm—with PMA

A person without enthusiasm is like a watch without a mainspring. Father John O'Brien, research professor of theology at the University of Notre Dame, says, "the first ingredient which I believe is absolutely necessary for a successful, efficient, and competent individual is enthusiasm." He adds, "Enthusiasm comes from the Greek words that let you look into the root of this word—into its basic, fundamental and original meaning. The first is *theos*, which means God. The other two words are *en-Tae,* so that in the early usage of this term of the ancient Greeks, it literally meant, 'God within you.'" Further: "No battle of any importance can be won without enthusiasm."

To become enthusiastic about achieving a desirable goal, keep your mind on that goal day after day. The more worthy and desirable your objectives, the more dedicated and enthusiastic you will become. Understand and act on William James's statement: "The emotions are not always immediately subject to reason *but they are always immediately subject to ACTION*" (emphasis added). Enthusiasm thrives on a positive mind and positive action. This is the key to controlling your enthusiasm: always give it a worthy goal to focus on and once you have channeled it toward that goal, it will carry you forward.

Real enthusiasm comes from within. However, enthusiasm is like getting water from a well; first you have to prime the pump but soon the water flows and flows and flows. You can be enthusiastic about everything and anything you know or do. Enthusiasm is a PMA characteristic. It can be generated naturally from one's thoughts, feelings and emotions, but more important, it can be generated at will.

TO BE ENTHUSIASTIC . . . ACT ENTHUSIASTICALLY!

My commitment to use the principle in my life is:

_____

_____

_____

_____

9. Enforce SELF-DISCIPLINE—with PMA

Self-discipline enables you to develop control over yourself. Self-discipline begins with mastery of your thoughts, what you really are, what you really do. Your failures and your successes are the results of habits. We are creatures of habit, but because we are minds with bodies, we can change our habits.

Self-discipline is perhaps the most important function in aiding an individual in the development and maintenance of habits of thought which enable that person to fix his or her entire attention upon any desired purpose and to hold it there until that purpose has been attained.

If you do not control your thoughts, you do not control your deeds. Think first and act afterward. Self-discipline is the principle by which you may voluntarily shape the patterns of your thoughts to harmonize with your goals and purposes.

DIRECT YOUR THOUGHTS, CONTROL YOUR EMOTIONS, ORDAIN YOUR DESTINY WITH PMA.

My commitment to use this principle in my life is:

_____

_____

_____

_____

10. THINK ACCURATELY—with PMA

Accurate thinking is based on two major fundamentals:

1. Inductive reasoning, based on the assumption of unknown facts or hypotheses.
2. Deductive reasoning, based on known facts or what are believed to be facts.

In school we are taught deductive and inductive reasoning and the fallacy that results in starting with the wrong premise in the one instance and making the wrong inference in the other. Accurate thinking and common sense are in part the result of experiences. You can learn from your own experiences as well as those of others when you learn how to recognize, relate, assimilate, and apply principles in order to achieve your goals.

1. Separate facts from fiction or hearsay evidence.
2. Separate facts into classes: important and unimportant.

Be careful of others' opinions. They could be dangerous and destructive. Make sure your opinions are not someone else's prejudices. The accurate thinker learns to use his or her own judgment and to be cautious no matter who may endeavor to influence him or her.

TRUTH WILL BE TRUTH REGARDLESS OF A CLOSED MIND, IGNORANCE, OR REFUSAL TO BELIEVE.

My commitment to use this principle in my life is:

_____
_____
_____
_____

11. Control YOUR ATTENTION—with PMA

Controlled attention is organized mind power. It is the highest form of self-discipline. Controlled attention is the act of coordinating all the faculties of the mind and directing their combined power to a given end or definite objective. It is an act that can be obtained only by the strictest sort of self-discipline.

It is obvious, therefore, that when you voluntarily fix your attention upon a definite major purpose of a positive nature and force your mind through your daily habits of thought to dwell on the subject, you condition your subconscious mind to act on that purpose. Controlled attention, when it is focused upon the object of your definite major purpose, is a medium by which you make positive application of the principle of suggestion.

The mind never remains inactive, not even during sleep. It works continuously by reactions to the influences which reach it. Therefore, the object of controlled attention is that of keeping your mind busy with thought material which may be helpful in attaining the object of your desire.

Controlled attention is self-mastery of the highest order, for it is an accepted fact that the person who controls his or her own mind may control everything else.

> **KEEP YOUR MIND ON THE THINGS YOU WANT AND OFF THE THINGS YOU DON'T WANT.**

My commitment to use this principle in my life is:

_____

_____

_____

_____

12. Inspire TEAMWORK—with PMA

Teamwork is a willing cooperation and the coordination of effort to achieve a specific objective. When the spirit of teamwork is willing, voluntary, and free, it leads to the attainment of great and enduring power.

It is a system which coordinates all the team players' resources and talents and automatically discourages dishonesty and unfairness, while it adequately compensates the individuals who serve honestly and unselfishly.

The principle of teamwork differs from the mastermind principle in that it is based on the coordination of effort without necessarily embracing the principle of definiteness of purpose or the principle of harmony, two important essentials of the mastermind.

Teamwork produces power, but the question of whether the power is temporary or permanent depends on the motive that inspired the cooperation. If the motive is one that inspires people to cooperate willingly, the power produced by this sort of teamwork will endure as long as that spirit of willingness prevails.

Teamwork builds individuals and businesses and provides unlimited opportunity for all. It is sharing a part of what you have—a part that is good—with others.

> THAT WHICH YOU SHARE WILL MULTIPLY;
> THAT WHICH YOU WITHHOLD WILL DIMINISH.

My commitment to use this principle in my life is:

_____

_____

_____

_____

13. Learn from ADVERSITY AND DEFEAT— with PMA

Every adversity carries with it the seed of an equivalent or greater benefit for those who have PMA and apply it.

Defeat may be a stepping-stone or a stumbling block, according to your mental attitude and how you relate it to yourself.

It is never the same as failure unless and until it has been accepted as such.

Your mental attitude in respect to defeat is the factor of major importance which determines whether you ride with tides of fortune or misfortune. The person with a positive mental attitude reacts to defeat in the spirit of determination not to accept it. The person with a negative mental attitude reacts to defeat in the spirit of hopeless acceptance.

> THE WORST THING THAT HAPPENS TO YOU MAY BE
> THE BEST THING THAT CAN HAPPEN TO YOU IF YOU
> DON'T LET IT GET THE BEST OF YOU.

My commitment to use this principle in my life is:

_____

_____

_____

_____

14. Cultivate CREATIVE VISION—with PMA

Man's greatest gift is his thinking mind. It analyzes, compares, chooses. It creates, visualizes, foresees, and generates ideas.

Imagination is your mind's exercise, challenge, and adventure. It is the key to all of a person's achievements, the mainspring of all human endeavor, the secret door to the soul of a person. Imagination inspires human endeavor in connection with material things and ideas associated with material things.

Imagination is the workshop of the human mind, where old ideas and established facts may be assembled into new combinations and put to new uses. It is the act of constructive intellect in the grouping of materials, knowledge, or thoughts into new, original, and rational systems, a constructive or creative faculty embracing poetic, artistic, philosophical, scientific, and ethical imagination.

Creative vision may be an inborn quality of the mind or an acquired quality, for it may be developed by the free and fearless use of the faculty of imagination.

Creative vision extends beyond interest in material things. It judges the future by the past and concerns itself with the future more than with the past. Imagination is influenced and controlled by the powers of reason and experience. Creative vision pushes these aside and attains its ends by basically new ideas and methods.

One of the ways to increase your flow of ideas is by developing the habit of taking study time, thinking time, and planning time. Be quiet and motionless, and listen for that small, still voice that speaks from within as you contemplate the ways in which you can achieve your objectives.

WHAT CAN BE CONCEIVED CAN BE CREATED——WITH PMA.

My commitment to use this principle in my life is:

_____

_____

_____

_____

15. Maintain SOUND HEALTH—with PMA

You are a mind with a body. Inasmuch as your brain controls your body, recognize that sound physical health demands a positive mental attitude, a health consciousness. Establish good, well-balanced health habits in work, play, rest, nourishment, and study. To maintain a health consciousness, think in terms of good physical health, not in terms of illness or disease. Remember, what your mind focuses upon, your mind brings into existence, whether it is financial success or physical health.

To maintain a positive attitude for the development and

maintenance of a sound health consciousness, use self-discipline, keep your mind free of negative thoughts and influence, and create and maintain a well-balanced life. Follow work with play, mental effort with physical effort, seriousness with humor, and you will be on the road to good health and happiness.

A sound mind and a sound body are attainable if you will put PMA to work for you. Remember, you can enjoy good health and live longer with PMA.

I FEEL HEALTHY! I FEEL HAPPY! I FEEL TERRIFIC!

My commitment to use this principle in my life is:
_____
_____
_____
_____

16. Budget your TIME AND MONEY— with PMA

Intelligently balance your use of time and resources, both business and personal. Take inventory of yourself and your activities so that you discover where and how you are spending your time and your money.

Engage in study, thinking, and planning time.

Don't waste your time or your money. Ten percent of all you earn is yours to keep and invest. Like any good business, budget your money. Use your time wisely toward attainment of your objectives. Develop a plan for the use of your income for expenses, savings, and investments.

YOU DON'T ALWAYS GET WHAT YOU EXPECT
UNLESS YOU INSPECT—WITH PMA.

My commitment to use this principle in my life is:

_____

_____

_____

_____

17. Use COSMIC HABITFORCE—with PMA

Cosmic habitforce pertains to the entire universe and is the law by which the equilibrium of the universe is maintained through established patterns or habits. It is the law which forces every living creature and every particle of matter to come under the dominating influence of its environment, including the physical habits and thought habits of humankind.

Cosmic habitforces are the powers which you apply with PMA when you use the universal laws or principles. Cosmic habitforces are employed when you use your mind powers whether they pertain to your conscious or subconscious mind. That is how you think and grow richer or achieve anything in life you desire (in principle) that doesn't violate the laws of God or the rights of your fellowman.

All of us are ruled by habits. These are fastened upon us by repeated thoughts and experiences. You have complete right of control over your thoughts. We create patterns of thought by repeating certain ideas or behavior until the Law of Cosmic Habitforce takes over those patterns and makes them more or less permanent unless or until you consciously rearrange them.

Habits: You have them—some good, perhaps others bad. Many you are aware of, but some that are undesirable you are blinded to. Each begins in your mind consciously or subconsciously. And each can be developed and neutralized or changed at will through the proper use of your mind. You have this power.

You are ruled by your habits. It takes a habit to replace a

habit. Develop positive habits that will be in harmony with the achievement of your definite purpose or goal.

> SOW AN ACT, AND YOU REAP A HABIT.
> SOW A HABIT, AND YOU REAP A CHARACTER.
> SOW A CHARACTER, AND YOU REAP A DESTINY.

My commitment to use this principle in my life is:

_____

_____

_____

ACKNOWLEDGMENTS

Many people were very helpful to me in editing this book. I am particularly grateful for the inspiration of two men who knew Napoleon Hill well and whose words reinforced his: W. Clement Stone and Michael J. Ritt.

There are many people, organizations, and publications dedicated to promoting the philosophy of success; in addition to those mentioned in the text, I found the following particularly helpful in selecting examples that highlighted the wisdom of Napoleon Hill's advice: *Audacity, Entrepreneur, Working Woman, Smart Money, Sales and Marketing Management, The New Yorker,* and *Minorities and Women in Business* magazines; *The Walls Around Us* by David Owen; Michael Mahana of Smith Barney, Shearson.

Upon request, the reader may receive an autographed bookplate bearing the signature of the author. Address your request to the Napoleon Hill Foundation, 1440 Paddock Drive, Northbrook, IL 60062, and enclose a large, self-addressed, stamped envelope. With this bookplate you will receive a copy of one of Dr. Hill's famous success essays.

INDEX